SAIL, STEAM and SPLENDOUR

A Picture History
of Life Aboard
the Transatlantic Liners

SAIL, STEAM and SPLENDOUR

Byron S. Miller

With a Foreword by Frank O. Braynard

NYT 𝕮imes BOOKS

Staff for this book:

Writer and Editor
  Thomas Froncek

Designer
  James S. Ward

Coordinating Editor
  Edward H. Mahoney

Picture Editor
  Margaretta Barton Colt

Editorial Assistant
  William Waters

Design Assistants
  Tony Kluck
  Lou Scolnik

European Research
  Carol Glass-Storyk, England
  Kate Lewin, France and Germany

Additional Text and Captions
  Wendy Murphy
  Jane Polley
  David Thomson

Lithographic Engravings
  Dichroic Color Inc.

Library of Congress Catalog Card Number: 76–9732
International Standard Book Number: 0–8129–0638–1

This book is dedicated to
my father, Byron DeWitt Miller
and my mother, Hortense Strongman Miller

Contents

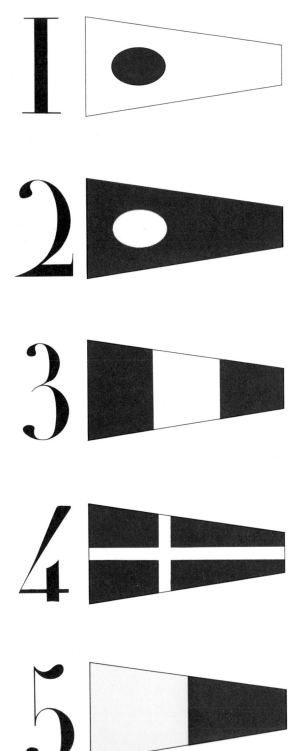

Foreword: A Century and a Half of History

Imagine four Waldorf Astorias linked together, subjected to the roll and pitch of the sea. Picture such a unit lashed to a 100,000 horsepower plant and built to stand the vibration of four screws turning at 180 revolutions per minute. Then imagine such a leviathan steaming through the worst gales and iceberg-infested sea lanes at top speeds.

Such were the great liners of the North Atlantic, the wonders of their age. Monuments of human engineering, these marvelously complex sea vehicles evolved over less than two centuries from awkward-looking adaptations of sailing ships to sleek grey-hounds and great floating cities. They were the largest man-made creations capable of motion.

Moreover, the gallant liners, large and small, played a crucial role in the social history of a continent. Without them, the New World could not have become so vastly populated in such a short time. Their story demands an important place in the annals of our Bicentennial United States.

As of this writing, the last of these floating mastodons are still with us. The *France,* while idle, is still "in being." The *QE2* is still in service. But it is safe to say, however reluctantly, that no more ocean giants will ever be laid down. And when they are all gone, how will future generations be able to picture them? Strangely, the best-remembered liners of the future may be such craft as the *Andrea Doria,* the *Lusitania,* and the mighty *Titanic.* They are there, intact, on the bottom of the ocean floor. Perhaps one day a thousand years from now, they will be raised. And what mind-boggling artifacts they will be!

Technical changes, advances in design and engineering, and social changes over the past two centuries have meant a rapid turnover for ocean liners. What was startlingly new one year was old-fashioned ten or fifteen years later, giving a liner an average life span of less than twenty years.

During the evolution of the liner, for instance, three basic materials were used for hull construction. The first sailing ships with steam engines were built of wood. Then, with the famous *Great Britain,* launched in 1843, came iron, and finally steel.

With propulsion there were also three basic evolutionary changes. First came ships using sail and side paddle wheels (the stern wheels used on riverboats were more efficient but less maneuverable in rough water). Then came the use of propeller and sails, for sails could not be abandoned as long as there was a chance of an engine breakdown or a screw shaft being broken. Finally, the development of the twin-screw vessel provided insurance against complete mechanical failure, and so freed steamships from the vagaries of the wind.

These technological changes did not occur all at once. The three types of hull construction and the three types of propulsion overlapped and in many ships were combined. The *Great Eastern,* launched in 1858, had an iron hull and wooden superstructure, boasted six masts and many sails, had two monster paddle wheels, and a twenty-four-foot propeller. The use of sails continued right up to the twentieth century. In the specifications for the quadruple-screw *Vaterland* (launched in 1913), it was spelled out that her masts "were not to be fitted for sails."

Rapid engineering developments kept putting the finest of the Atlantic liners out of date. How could the British outdo the two giant four-cylinder, three-crank, quadruple expansion engines put into Germany's *Kaiser Wilhelm II* of 1903? But even as these engines, the most powerful reciprocating steam engines ever built for a ship, were proudly delivering the bulk of the passenger trade to the ship's owners, a brand new device was evolving: the steam turbine. How could anyone surpass the vast power plant of the 1914 *Bismarck,* with her forty-seven boilers occupying two-thirds of her hull? Yet today's *Queen Elizabeth 2,* with more horsepower, runs on just three boilers.

The changes in creature comforts aboard the Atlantic liners have been equally striking and demonstrate that there really has been progress in man's humanity to his fellow man. Emigrants on the first Atlantic steamships were subjected, as these pages will show, to the most frightful conditions. Their very lives were sometimes sacrificed in the attempt to reach the New World in vile pens little better than those on slave ships.

But then, thanks to enlightened shipowners and the highly competitive nature of the passenger trade, there were improvements: better sanitary facilities, clean bunks, the provision and cooking of food, better ventilation, and more privacy. Eventually, there were even some "luxuries" for the emigrant. A widely publicized luxury on the pre-World War I ships of the Hamburg-America Line was a nice big room filled with white enameled washtubs, where emigrants could wash their clothes.

Meanwhile, those traveling in cabin or first class enjoyed the very finest luxuries the size of the ship could permit, from full-length mirrors on the *Savannah* to sea green, shell-encrusted spitoons on the Collins Line's *Baltic,* to the three-deck-high Pompeian swimming pool on the *Imperator.*

The internal changes brought outward adaptations and radical modifications to the silhouette of the Atlantic liner. The fat stubby hull became thinner and then broadened in comparison to the ship's length, as the experience of naval architects brought a better understanding of what was needed to insure maximum speed and safety. The clipper bow, so long and proudly boasted on sailing craft, was abandoned and then, with the *Normandie,* brought back into style, until today's cruise liners have even more extreme clipper bows than any clippers ever had. The bowsprit was lost forever, and the masts became little more than flagpoles and radar towers.

As might be expected, the smokestack, proudest badge of all in steamship styling, has always been the chief identifying feature of the Atlantic liner, from the crooked, swivel stack of the *Savannah* to the phallic funnel of the *QE2.* Bedecked with a fantastic variety of heraldic emblems and color schemes, the stacks show a wonderful history of change. There have been square stacks, and stacks as tall as the masts to raise the smoke above the sails. There have been three, four, and even a five-stacked liner, and there were a few daring, but unsuccessful, experiments in building ships with no stacks at all. Now the trend is toward one huge funnel far aft.

All these changes help to explain why the average liner has had such a short life. How sad to see such masterpieces go to the scrapyard so quickly! Like the pyramids and the cathedrals, the great ocean liners deserve to be remembered as tremendous achievements. They were monuments to highly developed skills, to the men who built them and who commanded them, to the crews that served aboard them, and to the passengers who first dared to sail in a ship that had "a fire aboard" (as the early steamships were described).

The pride of size, the competitive joy of building a speed queen, and the gallantry of good performance all meant much in the evolution of the steamship and in the flowering of the mechanical age on the world's premier sea lane, the North Atlantic.

FRANK O. BRAYNARD

Past President of the Steamship Historical Society of America

Preface: A Personal Note

The idea of compiling a picture history of the North Atlantic steamships has been in my mind for a long time. It has become more timely as the great ships have been withdrawn from service. Indeed, halfway through the preparation of this book, my wife and I took what unexpectedly turned out to be the last crossing of the *France,* one of the last great liners.

The liners that have plied the Atlantic between Europe and America during the past one hundred fifty years have not been slighted by historians. Many knowledgeable books have been written about their technical and navigational aspects and about their place in social history. Many of these books include wonderful stories and descriptive details.

What has been lacking, however, has been an illustrated history: a book that would show the liners themselves, in all their magnificence and power; a book that would bring the reader face-to-face with the engineering geniuses who designed the great liners, the visionaries who built them, the men and women who worked on them, and the diverse people who traveled on them; a book, most of all, that would allow the reader to see and to share the experience of crossing the Atlantic in a steamship.

This is the kind of book I have tried to compile, with the help of a talented crew of editors and researchers. Drawing on a wealth of material provided by museums; picture libraries, and private collections in the United States, Canada, and Europe, we examined thousands of illustrations.

What we looked for were pictures of what a passenger would see on deck, in his cabin, in the grand saloon, and in the engine room; pictures that would illustrate the changing social customs aboard ship, the life of the emigrants at sea, improvements in accommodations, and advances in marine technology. Whenever possible, we tried to find pictures that have never before been reproduced. For every one of the book's more than six hundred illustrations, at least a dozen were examined and discussed. In the end, many extraordinary pictures had to be discarded.

My own impressions of life aboard the steamships go back to my childhood. My father worked in England but was required to report to his home office in New York every year. So I was traveling back and forth across the Atlantic from a very early age. (I still remember the time when, as a boy, I slid down the railing of the grand staircase shown on page 144.) Then, and in later years, I had the good fortune to cross on many of the great ships shown in this book. And the memories of those crossings in the years between the wars are still vivid in my mind.

Preparations for a voyage were complex, and there was always confusion at the pier . . . "Where are the bags?" . . . "Good-bye." . . . "Don't forget to write me." . . . "Good Luck." . . . "Bon Voyage!"

Then the huge black and white riveted wall that you glimpsed only momentarily from the pier begins to throb. . . . There's the repeated cry, "All ashore that's going ashore!" . . . And the bellow and enormous white blast of the ship's great steam horns announce the start of her three thousand mile voyage. . . .

Kisses, confetti, and sometimes streamers are thrown from the rail to the waving crowd on the dock. The turbines begin to spin, the reduction gears engage and, "slow astern," the ship backs out into the river. Many tugs help her turn, but once turned and outward bound she is a greyhound on her own.

A day: late breakfast in your cabin, a stroll on deck, lazy reading or dozing in your named deck chair, sunning or deck games, people-watching. At eleven o'clock, bouillon and crackers. Later, a splendid lunch, more relaxation and deck games, reading, or writing long-overdue notes. And then tea, with assorted goodies. A swim, cards, new-found acquaintances. But above all, rest and peace of mind.

Even the severe winter storms fascinated me: the excitement of the rolling and plunging ship, the sight of the bow rising and falling into green water, the wind-driven water surging back over the foredeck.

In the evening, calm or storm, it came time to dress for dinner. A fine menu, faultlessly served, was often followed by a movie or dance, which led up to my favorite nightly activity: the ship's Auction Pool. Every day the captain would announce the probable miles to be covered from noon to noon. The chief smoking-room steward would ask a prominent passenger to auction each mile from one to ten around the captain's estimate. High and low fields were also sold. The odds against winning were pretty long. I only won once in some forty crossings. But it was all good fun.

For me, the most cherished time and mood came during the evening hours, as dusk covered the sea and you stood forward on the sun deck. The sky turned from red to deep blue to black, the wind hummed through the rigging, and you saw the forms of the masts and giant funnels turn black to meet the sky. . . . These were the times to remember.

I sincerely hope you enjoy looking at this book as much as we have enjoyed compiling it. Whether you recall your own crossings, or learn for the first time the excitement of the great liners, these pictures convey the drama of the Steamship Age in a way that words alone never can.

To the crew that made this book possible, I would like to extend my deepest appreciation: to Thomas Froncek, our writer and editor; to James Ward, our designer; to our picture editor, Margaretta Barton Colt, and to her assistants overseas, Carol Glass-Storyk in London and Kate Lewin in Paris; to William Waters, our researcher and picture cataloguer; and to Roger Jellinek at Quadrangle/ The New York Times Book Company. Particularly I want to thank my overall coordinator on this project, Edward H. Mahoney, for his guidance and good council.

Byron S. Miller
Norwalk, Connecticut

Steam Conquers the Atlantic

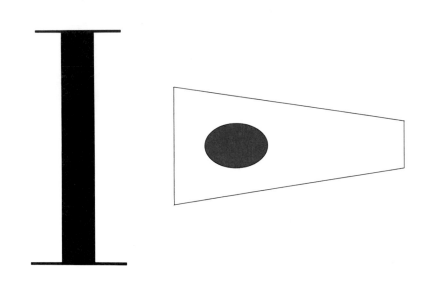

1819–1838

The Atlantic's broad horizon is clouded for the first time by steamship smoke when the square-rigger *Savannah* crosses eastward in the spring of 1819, using paddle wheels and a steam engine as well as wind and sail. . . . Despite the *Savannah*'s success and the rising popularity of river steamers, few people are ready to trust their lives or their cargo to an ocean-going vessel with a volcano burning in its bowels. . . . However experiments with steam continue. . . . And by 1838, the *Sirius* and the *Great Western* run the first great transatlantic steamship race, for the honor and profit of being the first to cross entirely under steam.

The *Savannah* is shown here in the only known contemporary engraving. The miniature of her captain, Moses Rogers, was painted in St. Petersburg (now Leningrad), where Rogers tried unsuccessfully to find a buyer for the ship.

What appeared to be a ship on fire was spotted off the southernmost tip of Ireland on the morning of June 17, 1819. There she was, with sails furled and with a long column of smoke and sparks spouting from her midships. Sent to the rescue, the *Kite,* one of the King's revenue cutters, came speeding on under full sail.

But to the surprise of those aboard the *Kite,* the swift cutter was unable to catch up with the smoking ship. It took a warning shot across her stern to bring her to a halt, and only then did it become clear that the ship had been in no danger at all. On the contrary, the little soot-spewing vessel had just ushered in a new age of sea travel. The *Savannah,* named after her home port in America and fitted with an engine and side paddlewheels, had just become the first ship to cross the Atlantic—or any other ocean—using steam as well as the traditional wind power.

The *Savannah*'s historic voyage came at a time when mail- and passenger-carrying packet ships had just begun making regularly scheduled crossings between Europe and America, casting off at the appointed hour whether or not they were full and no matter what the weather. Such crossings still took about twenty-three days eastward and some forty days westward, against the prevailing winds; but at least merchants and travelers could rely on regular departure times and fairly regular arrivals.

It was also a time when steamboats were becoming a familiar sight on the rivers of Europe and North America. Ever since a Devonshire blacksmith named Thomas Newcomen had built the first primitive steam engine in 1705, inventors had been seeking ways of applying steam power to navigation so that sea travel could be independent of the direction of the wind and tide.

Inventors' imaginations were stirred anew when, in the 1770s, a young Glasgow instrument maker, James Watt, devised a more efficient version of Newcomen's steam engine. Whereas the earlier machine had used steam to drive a piston up and atmospheric pressure to bring it back down again, in Watt's double-acting or "reciprocating" engine steam was introduced on both sides of the piston, offering greater power and efficiency.

The development of a practical steam engine was a major advance toward the Industrial Revolution. Indeed, the sooty mill towns of nineteenth-century Europe and America were testaments to the ingenuity of Thomas Newcomen and James Watt. And so were the long plumes of smoke that marked the growing preeminence of steam power on the rivers and oceans of the world.

The first time a double-acting engine was used successfully for navigation was in 1783, when a steamboat built by a French aristocrat, Marquis Claude de Jouffroy d'Abbans steamed upstream for fifteen minutes on the Saône. Lacking adequate financial backing, however, Jouffroy was prevented from making any further attempts, and France lost the opportunity to take the lead in the development of steam navigation.

In America, meanwhile, George Washington was recording in his diary (September 6, 1784) that he "was shown the model of a boat constructed by the ingenious Mr. Rumsey for ascending rapid currents by mechanism." The inventor of the boat, James Rumsey, was a Virginia shopkeeper whose experiments with steam propulsion roused the interest of a number of influential patrons, including Benjamin Franklin. Rumsey died when he was on the verge of developing a successful steamboat. By 1790, John Fitch, a Connecticut clockmaker, was operating a regular though short-lived steamboat service on the Delaware River.

Failures and partial successes did little to change the minds of those who, like Watt himself, doubted

The stern-wheeler (opposite) represents the earliest known attempt at steam navigation. Designed by Jonathan Hulls, an Englishman, in 1736, the boat was to be used for towing larger vessels in and out of port when the wind dropped or the tide was unfavorable. Hulls' attempt failed, but later improvements in steam engines enabled American John Fitch (right) to operate the first regular steamboat service, using a boat with three duckleg paddles (shown in the patent drawing below). Traveling in 1790 between Philadelphia and Trenton, the boat averaged seven miles per hour. But the stagecoach was faster, and Fitch was driven out of business. Fitch's screw propeller (far right) was less successful but no less ingenious.

John Fitch's Screw-propeller Steam-boat on the Collect, New York, 1796.

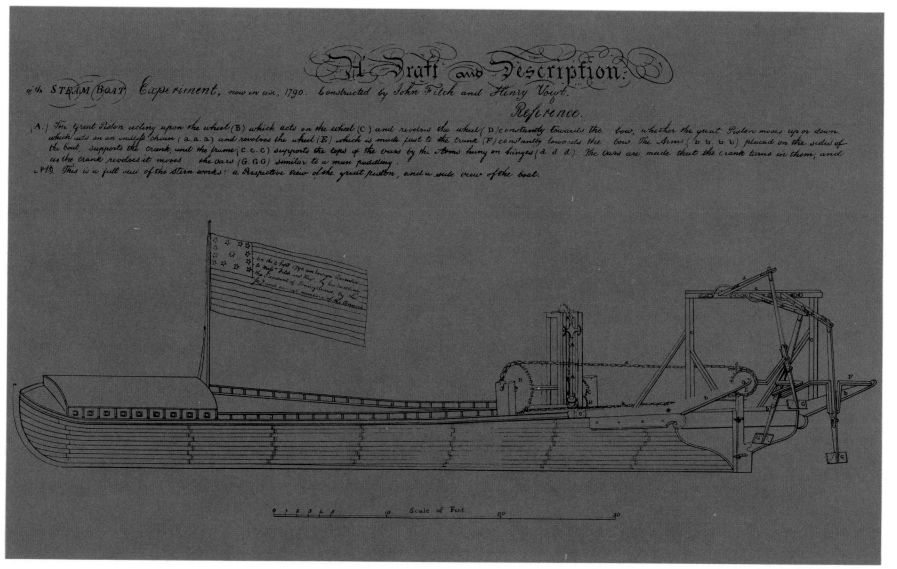

that steam navigation was practical. Some of the most acute objections to the idea were raised in 1803 by the prominent American architect Benjamin H. Latrobe in a scholarly paper:

First: the weight of the engine and of the fuel. *Second:* the large space it occupies. *Third:* the tendency of its action to rack the vessel, and render it leaky. *Fourth:* the expense of maintenance. *Fifth:* the irregularity of its motion, and the motion of the water in the boiler and the cistern, and of the fuel vessel in rough water. *Sixth:* the difficulty arising from the liability of the paddles and oars to break, if light, and from weight, if made strong.

These were very real problems; but one by one they were being solved by the pioneers of steam navigation. Just four years after Latrobe published his comments, the world had its first commercially successful steamboat: Robert Fulton's *North River Steam Boat,* famous to history as the *Clermont,* which began operating on the Hudson River in 1807. And by 1812, Henry Bell's *Comet,* the first successful steamer in Europe, was making regular trips up and down the Clyde, between Glasgow and Greenock, in Scotland.

It was still many years before a steam-powered vessel was ready to brave the open seas. But the steamship revolution had begun.

Robert Fulton's *North River Steam Boat,*
later called the *Clermont* (left), first came
chugging up the Hudson from New York
City in 1807. To the people of Albany
she seemed like "a monster moving on the
waters, defying winds and tides, and
breathing flames and smoke." Steaming
upstream at an average speed of five
miles per hour, the *Clermont* was powered
by the machinery opposite center: a
single cylinder engine driven by steam
from a twenty-foot-long copper boiler.
Despite her ominous first impression,
the *Clermont* was an immediate financial
success. She continued in service for seven
years, giving Fulton (who is shown in the
portrait above) the chance to build a whole
series of steamcraft.

The first sea-going steam vessels, the Scottish *Comet* (left) and the American *Phoenix* (left, below), were better suited to river than sea travel. The *Phoenix,* denied the Hudson River trade by Fulton's monopoly, was sent down the coast in 1808 to begin service on the Delaware. Repeated engine failures and the battering of the Atlantic made the journey a nightmare. Most of the trip had to be spent in coves and behind sand bars, avoiding the ocean's waves. The *Comet* successfully ran a regular service on the rivers of Scotland between 1812 and 1819 (using the engine shown at right with its builder, John Robertson). However, she was wrecked in a storm soon after inaugurating service along the coast.

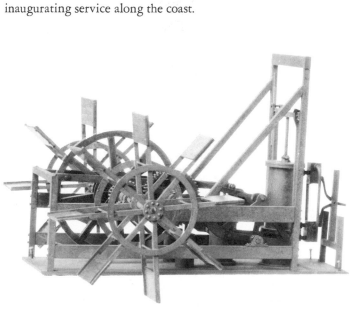

The "Spasmodic Pioneers" Brave the Atlantic Under Sail and Steam

"These 24 hours begins with light breezes and pleasant all Sail Set to the best advantage," wrote the sailing master in the entry (below) from the log of the *Savannah*'s voyage "towards Liverpool." (It would have been tempting fate to say a ship was sailing "to" its destination; "toward" was the best to be hoped for.) The logbook itself, shown at left only slightly larger than the original size, was bound in a scrap of canvas from the sail locker, its edges stitched and hemmed.

A "steam coffin," the *Savannah* was called by those who saw her being fitted out at her berth in a Manhattan shipyard. A trim sailing packet, she was a typical square-rigger. What made her unusual were the paddle wheels hung on her flanks, the elbowed chimney that stuck up between her masts, and the engine in her hold.

The *Savannah* was the first of what one marine historian has called the "spasmodic pioneers": sailing ships with auxiliary engines that crossed the Atlantic using steam for only part of the trip. The *Savannah,* setting out for Europe in May, 1819, used steam for only about one hundred hours of the almost thirty days she took to make the crossing. The rest of the time her collapsible paddle wheels were stored on deck and the ship proceeded under sail alone.

Like the *Savannah,* the few steam-auxiliaries that crossed the Atlantic in the 1820s—the British

Rising Star, the French *Caroline,* the Dutch *Curaçao* —relied mainly on sail and wind, using their engines only against headwinds, during periods of calm, or when entering and leaving port. Not one of them dared to cross the Atlantic by the stormy North Atlantic route. Instead, their owners chose the safer southern passage: to the Caribbean and to South America, where a mining boom was under way.

Not until 1833 did a ship appear to challenge the *Savannah*'s claim as the only steamer to cross the North Atlantic. She was the Canadian steam packet *Royal William,* built in Quebec and sent to London to be sold. The *Royal William* may not have steamed the whole way across, as her captain claimed, since sails had to be used when the engines were shut down every four days to clean the salt out of the boilers. But the ship was more of a steamer than any of her predecessors, and her crossing impressed shippers on both sides of the Atlantic.

Intended originally for the coastal passenger trade, the *Savannah,* shown here in a nineteenth-century painting (top), was fitted out "in the most tasty manner," according to one newspaper report. She had mahogany wainscoting, a profusion of mirrors, and berths for thirty-two passengers. Such finery must have been appreciated in the ship's home port, Savannah, Georgia, seen at right as it appeared in 1818, the year the Savannah Steam Ship Company was organized.

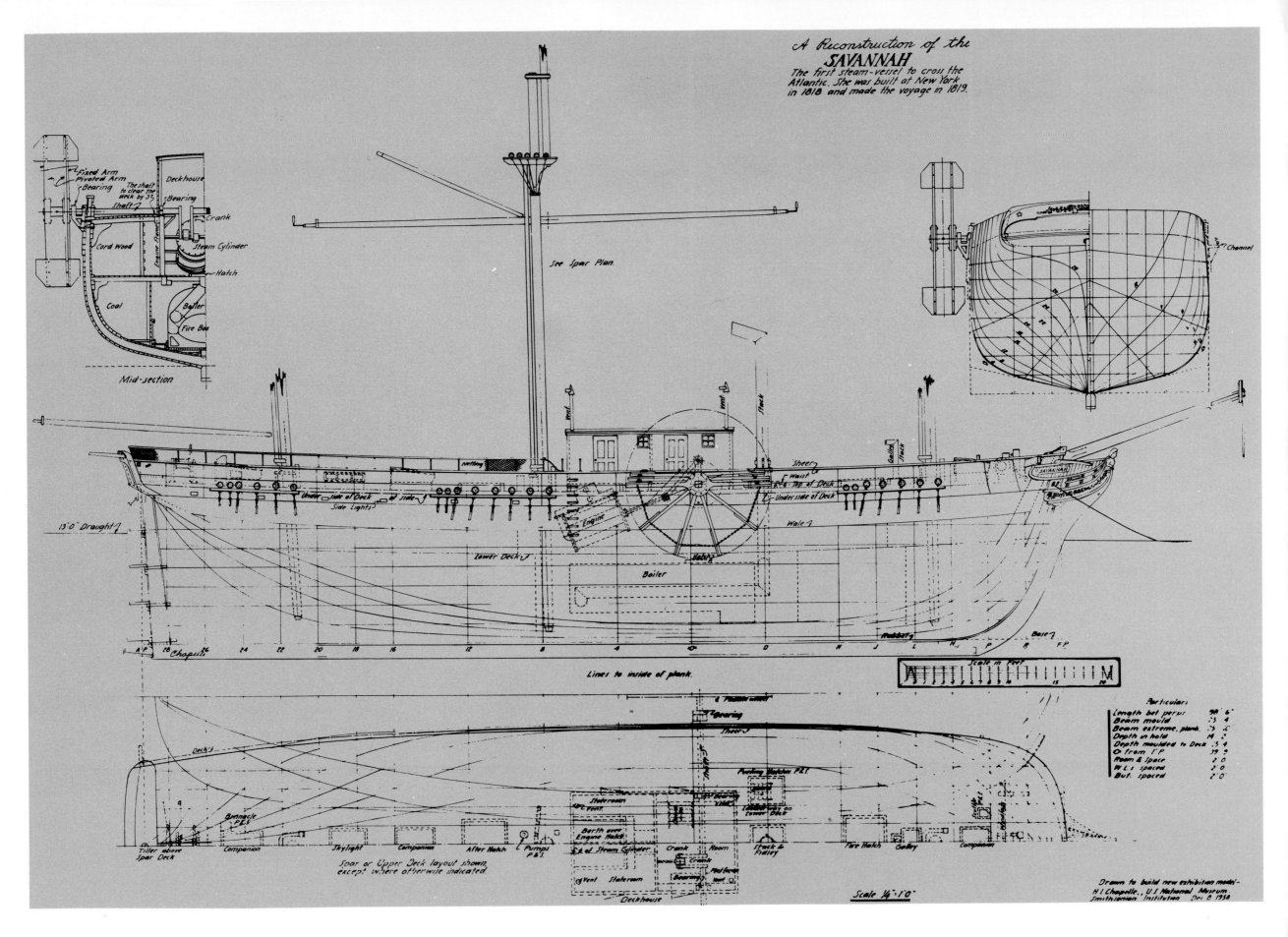

A Reconstruction of the
SAVANNAH
The first steam-vessel to cross the
Atlantic. She was built at New York
in 1818 and made the voyage in 1819.

Mid-section

Fixed Arm
Piveted Arm
Bearing
The shaft
to clear the
deck by 35
Shaft
Bearing
Deckhouse
Crank
Steam Cylinder
Hatch
Cord Wood
Coal
Boiler
Fire Box

See Spar Plan.

Channel

13'0" Draught

Side Lights
Under side of Deck
Side of Deck
Inside
Engine
Wale
Netting
Sheer
Waist
Top of Deck
Underside of Deck
Galley
Track
Vent
Vent
Track
Lower Deck
Boiler
Hatch
Rudder
Base

AP 28 Chapell 26 24 22 20 18 16 12 8 4 O D H J L N P R FP

Lines to inside of plank.

Scale in Feet

Particulars
Length bet perps ....
Beam mould ....
Beam extreme, plank ....
Depth in hold ....
Depth moulded to Deck ....
O from FP ....
Room & Space ....
W.L.s spaced ....
But. spaced ....

Deck'd
Binnacle P.&S.
Bearing
Sheer
Parting Valve P.&S.
Stateroom
Vent
Stateroom on Lower Deck
Bearing
Valve
Scuttle P.&S.
Berth over
Engine Hatch
St. of Steam Cylinder
Crank Crank Room
Track &
Fidley
Fore Hatch
Galley
Companion
Tiller above
Spar Deck
Companion
Skylight
Companion
After Hatch
Pumps
P.&S.
Vent Stateroom
Bearing
Malfarad
Vent

Deckhouse

Spar or Upper Deck layout shown,
except where otherwise indicated.

Scale ¼"=1'0"

Drawn to build new exhibition model -
H. I. Chapelle, U.S. National Museum
Smithsonian Institution Dec 6 1958

20

Based on contemporary descriptions, this modern reconstruction of the *Savannah* (opposite) shows how her engine, boiler, and collapsible paddle wheels may have been arranged. The drawing at top left shows how her fuel—coal and cordwood—may have been stored below decks.

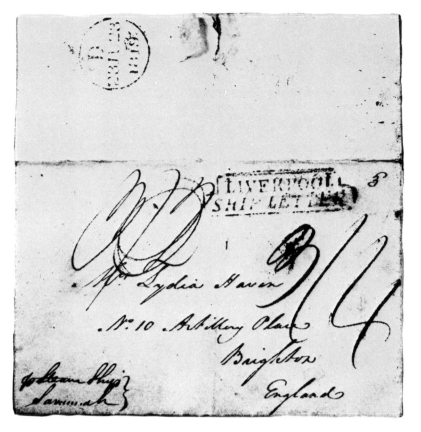

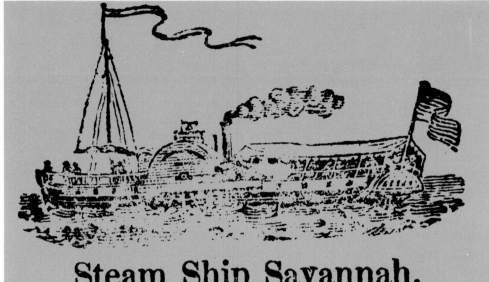

Steam Ship Savannah.

Will sail *THIS MORNING*, precisely at 9 o'clock, for CHARLESTON. For passage apply on board, at the Steam-Boat wharf.
April 14.

A new musical comedy, in ...o act... *My own Rival*, was produced on Monday night at this theatre. It is an agreeable little drama, with sufficient novelty of design to produce popularity for itself, and amusement to the public, at least for a short period.

The *Savannah* steam-vessel, recently arrived at Liverpool from America, the first vessel of the kind that ever crossed the Atlantic, was chased a whole day off the coast of Ireland, by the *Kite* revenue cruiser, on the Cork station, which mistook her for a ship on fire.

On Monday night a further respite was received at Newgate for *Thomas Bradbury*, under sentence of death for uttering for... Bank-not... during his R... H... ...nt's

"The Americans have beaten us on our own element," lamented an anonymous British observer after the *Savannah*'s arrival in Liverpool on June 20, 1819. Mementos of the voyage include a report from the London *Times* of the arrival (far left) and the only piece of mail known to have been carried on the trip (top left). The silver samovar (left) was presented to Captain Rogers by Lord Lynedoch, who was so impressed with the steamship that he booked passage on part of her voyage to St. Petersburg. A souvenir of an earlier voyage is the newspaper advertisement above. Illustrated with a river steamer, it touts the *Savannah*'s first trip with paying passengers: a journey from Savannah to Charleston in April, 1819.

The Rising Star,
_ Built under the direction of _
LORD COCHRANE

London Published 20th Sep. 1821

by A. Hudson &c. Cheapside

La Estrella Naciente,
Construida segun las direcciones del
LOR COCHRANE

upon the principle of Navigating either by Sails or by Steam the impelling Apparatus being placed in the Hold, and caused to operate through Apertures in the bottom of the Vessel.

Embarcacion de Vela ó de Vapor, cuya Maquina impulsiva, en la Bodega, obra por Aberturas en el fondo.

Using mostly sail, the *Rising Star* (above), built in Britain for use as a steam warship in the Chilean revolution, crossed the South Atlantic in 1822 and became the first steamer to enter the Pacific; but by the time she arrived in Chile the revolution was over. Using more wind than steam, the *Curaçao* (near left) made three crossings between Holland and Dutch Guiana in the late 1820s. The Canadian *Royal William* (far left) became the first ship to use steam for most of a crossing, setting out for London from Pictou, Nova Scotia, in 1833. Samuel Cunard, who later founded the Atlantic's most famous steamship line, was one of her backers.

The First Great Transatlantic Steamship Race: *Sirius* v. *Great Western*

A direct steam voyage from New York to Liverpool? "They might as well talk of making a direct voyage from New York or Liverpool to the moon," snorted a skeptic of the mid-1830s. Yet in the spring of 1838, not one but two vessels were racing across the Atlantic, each ship's captain determined to be the first to use steam power for the entire crossing.

The *Great Western* was one of these, 212 feet long and built like a man-of-war. She had double oak ribs and a hull sheathed in copper below the waterline. The first steamship to be built expressly for transatlantic travel, she was the brainchild of Isambard Kingdom Brunel, the chief engineer of Britain's Great Western Railway Company, who was already famous as "The Little Giant"—a builder of bridges, tunnels, and railroads.

The *Great Western*'s challenger was a ship two-thirds her size and half her tonnage, a small steamer named the *Sirius*. Built for service on the English Channel, she was chartered by a Connecticut Yankee named Junius Smith, who had his mind set on becoming the "Father of Ocean Steam Navigation."

The *Sirius* was outclassed by the *Great Western* in every respect: size, speed, power, and luxury. But she got the jump on her rival, leaving the coaling station at Cork, Ireland, on April 4, 1838, with forty passengers bound for New York. The *Great Western,* delayed by a fire in her hold, did not leave Bristol until four days later. She carried only eight passengers, the fire having caused fifty others to back out.

Leaving the spectators behind on the docks, the two ships churned their way across the ocean. The *Sirius,* bucking strong headwinds, pitched and tossed so much that some crewmen wanted to turn back. But her captain prevailed, and she arrived in New York safely on April 23. Her appearance caused tremendous excitement. "Nothing is talked of in New York but this *Sirius,*" wrote the correspondent of the *Morning Herald.*

The *Great Western,* despite her late start and no less boisterous seas, came into New York twelve hours after the *Sirius.* Although she had lost the race, she unquestionably proved her superiority by crossing in fifteen days and five hours, compared to the *Sirius*'s eighteen days and ten hours. In the long run, too, the *Great Western* outshone her rival; while the *Sirius* made only one more round-trip crossing before going back to the cross-channel service, the *Great Western* continued to run a regular service, averaging six round trips a year and crossing the Atlantic sixty-four times in all. No other early steamer achieved such a record.

Isambard Kingdom Brunel

Junius Smith

"No occurrence for a long time past has excited so stirring an interest on the river," reported the London *Times* on the *Great Western*'s maiden voyage departure. Shown being launched in the engraving above left, the ship had berths for 240 passengers. Her saloon—seventy-five feet long and decorated with murals and Gothic arches—was the largest room afloat. By contrast, the most distinguishing feature of the *Sirius* (above) was her figurehead of a leaping dog (opposite), representing the Dog Star Sirius. Yet to one observer, watching from the deck of a becalmed sailing ship, she approached "in gallant style with the speed of a hunter, while we were moving with the rapidity of an ox-cart loaded with marsh mud."

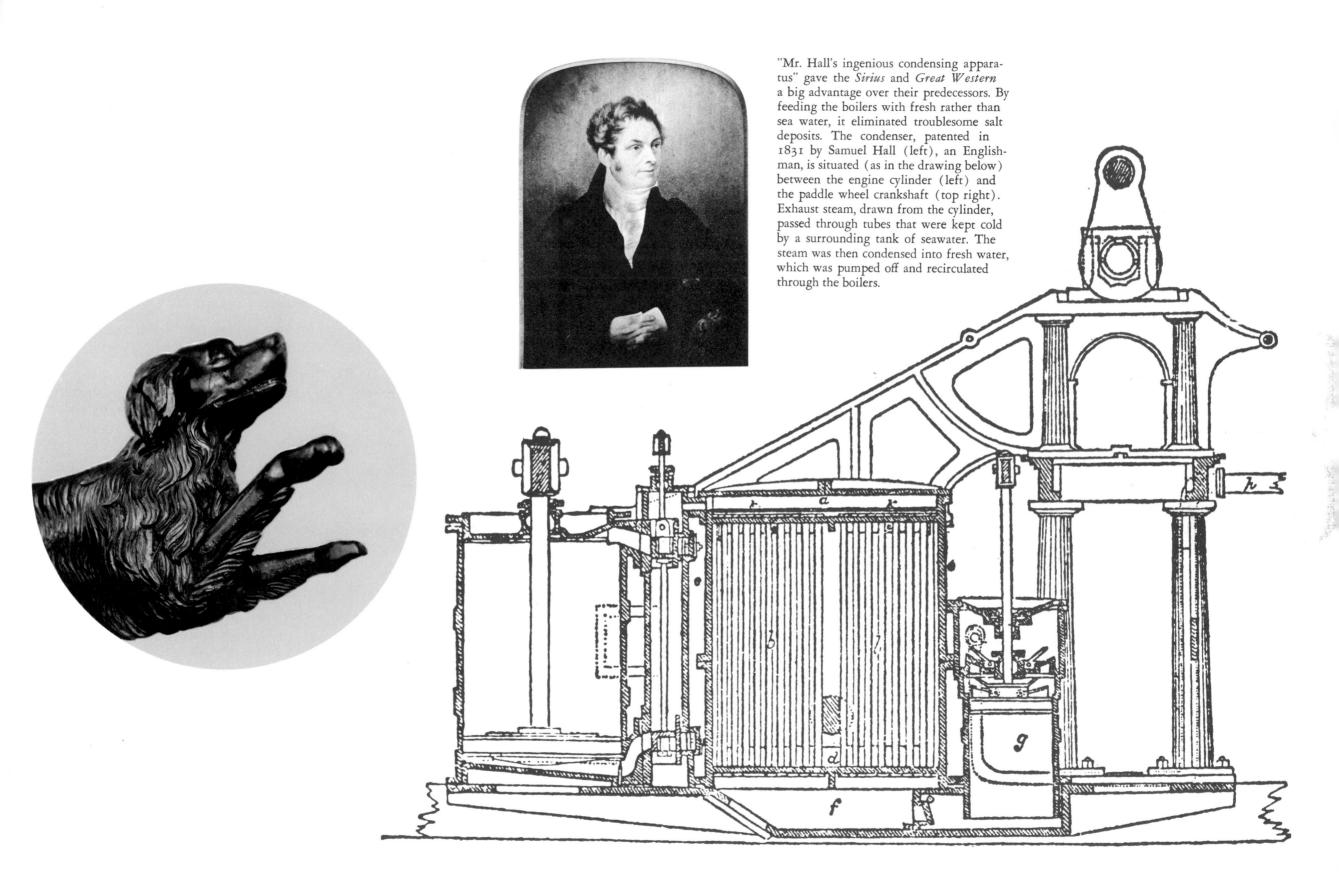

"Mr. Hall's ingenious condensing apparatus" gave the *Sirius* and *Great Western* a big advantage over their predecessors. By feeding the boilers with fresh rather than sea water, it eliminated troublesome salt deposits. The condenser, patented in 1831 by Samuel Hall (left), an Englishman, is situated (as in the drawing below) between the engine cylinder (left) and the paddle wheel crankshaft (top right). Exhaust steam, drawn from the cylinder, passed through tubes that were kept cold by a surrounding tank of seawater. The steam was then condensed into fresh water, which was pumped off and recirculated through the boilers.

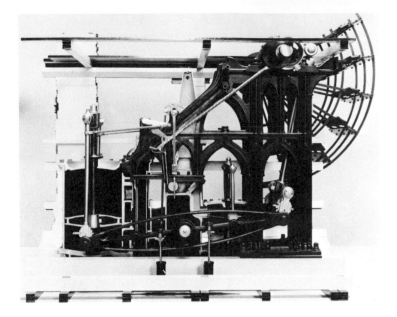

As celebrated in her heyday as the *Queen Mary* was to be in a later era, the *Great Western* had a march written in her honor (far right), dedicated to her captain. Whether the food on board was as spectacular as the ship is highly doubtful. Chops for breakfast and roasts for dinner were offered on the bill of fare (right), which perhaps made up in length for what it lacked in variety. A model of the kind of engine that drove the *Great Western* and most other early ocean steamers is shown above. Steam from a boiler drove the piston back and forth (bottom); connected to the piston was a crankshaft which turned the paddle wheel.

GREAT WESTERN STEAM SHIP

BILL OF FARE.

BREAKFAST.

Beefsteak Dishes
Mutton Chops
Pork Chops
Ham and Eggs
Fried Bacon
Fricasee Chicken
Veal Cutlets
Stews
Omelets
Boiled Eggs
Homony
Hash
Mush
Fried Fish
Broiled Chickens

DINNER.

Soups
Boiled Fish
Baked Fish
Roast Beef
Roast Mutton
Roast Lamb
Roast Turkey
Roast Veal
Roast Pork
Olive Ducks
Roast Fowls
Roast Geese
Boiled Mutton
"   Turkies
"   Fowls
Corned Beef
Corned Pork
Ham
Tongues
Fricandeau
Mutton Cutlets
Maccaroni
Curry
Irish Stew
Calves' Head

PASTRY.

Plum Pudding
Apple Dumpling
Raspberry Rollers
Apple Pudding
Apple Pies
Cranberry Pies
Raspberry "
Plum "
Mince "
Damson "
Cherry "
Rice Pudding
Maccaroni Pudding
Custard "

WINES.

GREAT WESTERN MARCH

Arranged and Respectfully

DEDICATED

to

Capt. James Hosken R.N.

Commander of the Great Western

by

CHARLES JARVIS.

Philadelphia, OSBOURN'S MUSIC SALOON, 30 S° Fourth St.

"The excitement yesterday was tremendous," began the New York *Morning Herald*'s report (right) of the completion of the first transatlantic steamship race on on April 23, 1838. The *Sirius,* which came in first, is shown entering New York Harbor in the picture at far right, bottom. When the *Great Western* arrived in New York a short time later—as shown in the detail (far right, top) from a painting of the period—her welcome outdid her rival's. A passenger described the scene: "Myriads seemed collected—boats had gathered around us in countless confusion, flags flying, guns were firing, and cheering again—the shore, the boats, on all hands around, loudly and gloriously, seemed as though they would never have done."

MORNING HERALD.

TUESDAY, APRIL 24, 1838.

Triumph of Steam--The Sirius and the Great Western--The passage of the Atlantic in fourteen days!

The excitement yesterday was tremendous; from an early hour in the morning until dark, myriads of persons crowded the Battery to have a glimpse of the first vessel which had crossed the Atlantic from the British isles, and arrived at this port; indeed, it is said, that every Englishman in the city, at one time or other, during the day, was gazing at the dark looking vessel with the American colors at the fore, and the flag of old England at the stern. This excitement was further increased by the arrival of the *Great Western*, from Bristol, which left that port on the 7th instant, making the passage in fifteen days, thus solving the problem of possibility, and showing what can be done by enterprize, expenditure, courage, and skill, in encountering the stormy weather which these two vessels have so successively braved and surmounted. The *Sirius*, however, is the pioneer, and to her the glory of the Argonaut is due.

The approach of the "Great Western" to the harbor, and in front of the Battery, was most magnificent. It was about four o'clock yesterday afternoon. The sky was clear—the crowds immense. The battery was filled with the human multitude, one half of whom were females, their faces covered with smiles, and their delicate persons with the gayest attire.— Below, on the broad blue water, appeared this huge thing of life, with four masts, and emitting volumes of smoke. She looked black and blackguard—as all the British steamers generally are—rakish, cool, reckless, fierce, and forbidding in their sombre colors to an extreme. As she neared the Sirius, she sla... ened her movements, and took a sweep round... ing a sort of half circle. At this moment... Battery sent forth a tumult... the revelation of...

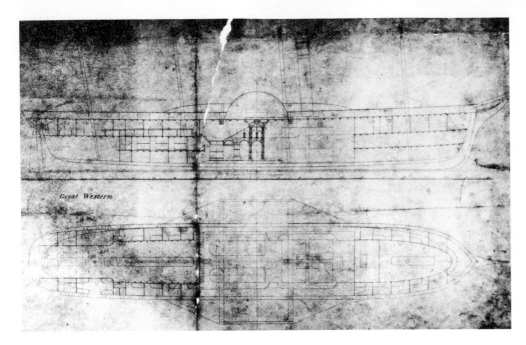

Like a mother whale surrounded by her calves, the *Great Western* is shown in this contemporary lithograph arriving in New York Harbor and being greeted by a crowd of river steamers and sailboats. A number of adventurous souls even braved the choppy water in rowboats. The contemporary drawings above show the ship's deck plan and, in the cutaway profile at top, the location of her engine and her steam-condensing apparatus.

Steam Fever

1838–1870

Victorian Gothic goes to sea . . . and Samuel Cunard gets his start with the help of a government mail subsidy. . . . The first Cunarders, "plain and comfortable" and with "nothing for show," make their mark and go unchallenged . . . until America's Collins Line enters the field, beating the competition with a fleet of swift and elegant steamships. . . . But the battle for supremacy ends in disaster for Collins, leaving the North Atlantic once again to the staunch Cunarders. . . . Meanwhile the *Great Britain*, the first iron-hulled, screw-driven steamship, puts to sea . . . and the mammoth *Great Eastern*, rises on its stocks—fifty years ahead of its time.

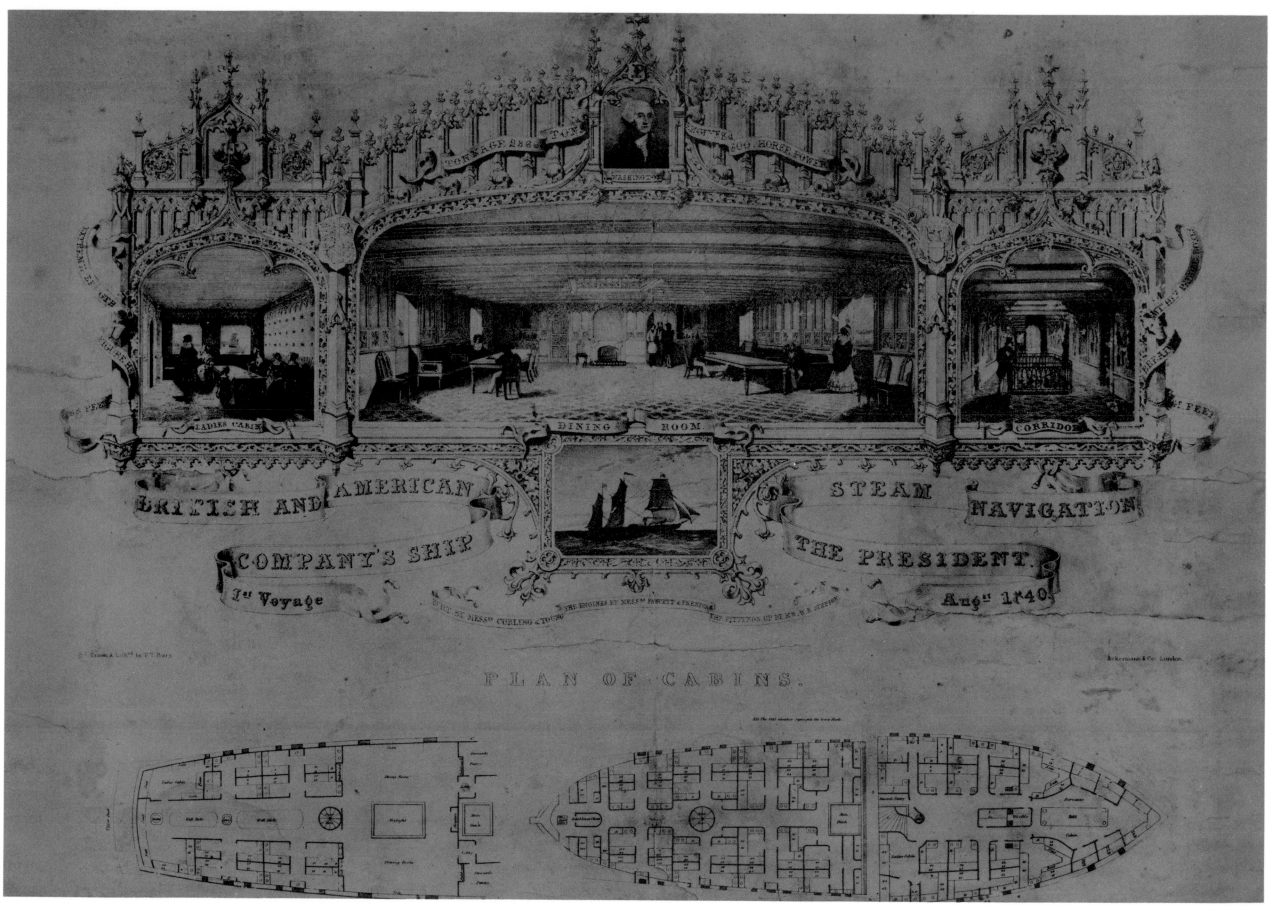

TONNAGE 2366 TON

WASHINGTON

500 HORSE POWER

LADIES CABIN

DINING ROOM

CORRIDOR

BRITISH AND AMERICAN

STEAM NAVIGATION

COMPANY'S SHIP

THE PRESIDENT.

1st Voyage

Augt 1840.

PLAN OF CABINS.

Neo-Gothic filigree frames views of the sumptuous interior of the *President*, launched in 1840 by the steamship pioneer Junius Smith.

"Steam vessels required for conveying Her Majesty's Mails and Despatches between ENGLAND and HALIFAX (Nova Scotia)," read an advertisement that appeared in the London newspapers in November, 1838. Impressed by the successes of the *Sirius* and *Great Western,* the British Admiralty was offering to subsidize a steamship line that could provide regular and rapid mail service with Britain's Canadian provinces. Logically, the owners of the *Sirius* and of the *Great Western* expected that one of them would win the contract. But they reckoned without knowledge of the shrewdness of a Halifax merchant named Samuel Cunard.

Cunard, who was spoken of as a "bright, tight little man with keen eyes, firm lips, and happy manners," was also known for his ability to make "both men and things bend to his will." As yet, he owned not a single steamship. But he was already the most prominent shipper in the largest British port in North America, and his sailing packets had been carrying the mails among the Maritime Provinces for nearly twenty-five years.

Intrigued by the possibilities of a transatlantic steamship service, Cunard proposed to run a fleet of "plain and comfortable" steamships from England to Halifax and back, twice each month, with a branch service to Boston. The British government liked the idea, and in 1839 Cunard was awarded the transatlantic mail contract and an annual subsidy of £55,000 (about $275,000). It was the beginning of a marriage which, for the better part of one hundred and forty years, was to make the North Atlantic almost a private preserve for the Cunard company and for Great Britain.

The mail-carrying contract was the reason for Cunard's longevity. Without it, fast, year-round steamship service simply did not pay. With rare exceptions, the multitude of steamship companies that sprang up in the years ahead quickly foundered without government support. A typical case was the line founded by E. K. Collins in the 1850s. The Collins Line was the only American company to offer Cunard any real competition and even held the speed record—the hypothetical "Blue Ribbon" which was already a coveted honor because fast crossings guaranteed a brisk business in first-class passengers and express cargo. But Collins stayed afloat only with the help of a U.S. mail subsidy; when that was withdrawn, the company collapsed.

The Americans fared no better than they did largely due to a lack of interest. In the 1830s and 1840s, America's pride lay in its sailing ships,

"Uncle John! Please send my letter to Cousin Jane in America for a penny," begs a little moppet of John Bull (right). The cartoon printed on the colored envelope on the opposite page were part of a propaganda campaign waged by businessmen and free trade advocates in the 1850s, who were trying to win cheaper transatlantic postage rates from both the British and American governments. But the cost of mailing a letter across the ocean remained well above a penny until the end of the nineteenth century. Stamp samples, like the one below, were issued to Cunard's captains in the early 1860s. They showed examples of transatlantic cancellation stamps then being used by the British Post Office.

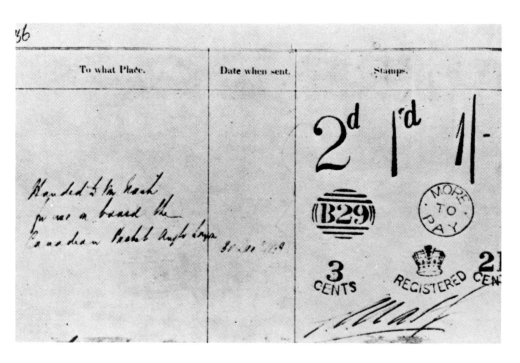

which were faster and cheaper than any others. So Americans were in no hurry to promote steam navigation. Besides, there was more poetry and romance in the billowing sails of a clipper ship than in the sooty mechanics of a steam packet.

More importantly, Americans in mid-century were looking not eastward toward Europe but were gazing westward toward their developing interior. For Americans, steam navigation meant mostly river navigation: wide, flat-bottomed boats with fast, high-pressure engines that carried immigrants and cargo to the western settlements.

Schemes for transatlantic steamship lines consequently won little support in America. Junius Smith discovered this for himself when he sought backing for the company that eventually sent the *Sirius* against the *Great Western*. "New Yorkers seem at times *stupid* about steam navigation," he wrote to a colleague. "How can they shut their eyes to the fact that steamships do (and have done for years) navigate the tempestuous coasts of Europe through the winter, at all seasons in all weather, whilst sailing ships lie in port."

But shut their eyes Americans did, and the British were not slow to press their advantage. One important British consideration was their keen interest in maintaining rapid communication with the distant reaches of the Empire by supporting a fleet of speedy "liners"—ships that left on schedule and made straight for their destination.

Then, too, Britons, from the very beginnings of their history, had always been concerned more with coastal and open-sea navigation than with river travel. Their early steamers were deep-draft vessels with high bulwarks, masts, and slow but steady low-pressure boilers; so the British readily made the transition to ocean travel.

Britain also benefited from having a head start in the Industrial Revolution. Coal and iron were plentiful, and mechanical skills well developed. By the late 1830s, Britain had produced both the steamship-building genius of the age, Isambard Kingdom Brunel, born in Portsmouth, and the foremost builder of marine engines, Robert Napier of Glasgow.

So it was to Britain that Junius Smith and Samuel Cunard turned in search of support: Smith to build the biggest and fastest liner in the world; Cunard to establish a reliable mail and passenger service. And although in coming decades other nations would enjoy success on the North Atlantic, more often than not the British would be in the lead.

Victorian Gothic Goes to Sea, and the *British Queen* Leads the Way

With flags flying and smoke pouring from her funnel, Junius Smith's *British Queen* (opposite) arrives off New York's Battery on her maiden voyage in 1839, a full year before rival Cunard's *Britannia* made her first trip. Smith's large and elegant ship— he boasted she was the "St. Paul's of naval architecture"—carried an appropriately regal figurehead (left) of Queen Victoria, in whose honor the ship had been named. The engine in Smith's 2,000-ton "floating colossus" was built by the Scottish engine-building genius Robert Napier (right), who had built the crankshaft of the pioneer *Royal William*, and who was soon after building Cunard's first four sister ships and the engines that propelled them across the Atlantic.

The victory of the *Sirius* over the *Great Western* boosted Junius Smith's hopes of becoming the "Father of Ocean Steam Navigation." But the achievement of his dream depended upon the success of the *British Queen,* launched in 1838, and of her consort, the *President,* launched nineteen months later. They were to be the largest ships afloat, each over 240 feet long, and were to run in tandem.

Delays in the building of her engines prevented the *British Queen* from entering the race against the *Great Western.* But once at sea, she proved a stiff competitor. "We have beat the *Great Western* every voyage this year," boasted her captain in 1840.

The *President* was elaborately furnished and decorated in the best early Victorian style and bore a bust of George Washington as her figurehead. But she was neither so fast nor so lucky as the *British Queen.* Having sailed from New York in March, 1841, on her third return voyage, the *President* was never heard from again.

The disaster hurt all steamers; Cunard's new company survived only because of its mail subsidy. But the blow fell most heavily on Smith's British & American Steam Navigation Company—already suffering from competition with Cunard, the firm could not survive the loss.

Junius Smith's second big paddlewheeler, the *President,* succumbs to mountainous waves in a Currier & Ives print (below) reconstructing the ship's fate. No evidence has ever been found explaining what befell the *President*—she vanished without a trace. But the Currier & Ives version was probably correct; the ship was last seen wallowing in a gale. A less likely explanation was the suggestion of a dime novel (below, right) that the *President* had been attacked by pirates. In any case, the loss was fatal to Smith's company and to his dream of fame, fortune, and a British knighthood. The company folded, the *British Queen* was sold to Belgium, and Smith retired to South Carolina where he devoted himself to horticulture.

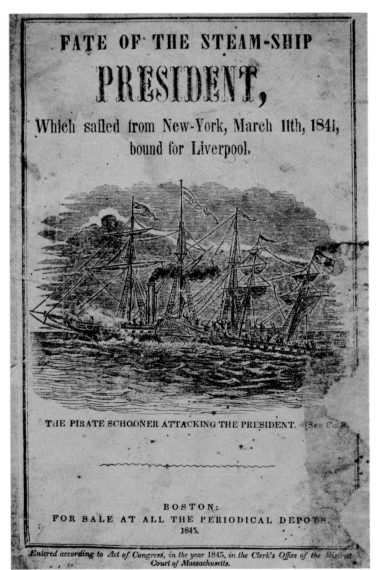

FATE OF THE STEAM-SHIP

PRESIDENT,

Which sailed from New-York, March 11th, 1841, bound for Liverpool.

THE PIRATE SCHOONER ATTACKING THE PRESIDENT. [See C. 8.

BOSTON:
FOR SALE AT ALL THE PERIODICAL DEPOTS.
1845.

Entered according to Act of Congress, in the year 1845, in the Clerk's Office of the District Court of Massachusetts.

The firm jaw, steady gaze and business-like air displayed in the portrait of Samuel Cunard (left) evidently impressed the members of the British government who awarded him the lucrative mail contract. Fifty years old when he founded his steamship line, Cunard was already a wealthy merchant and coastal shipping magnate in Halifax, Nova Scotia (below, left), where his Loyalist father had settled after the American Revolution. What made Cunard so successful in his steamship venture was that he had ordered Napier to build four sister ships; thus he could offer both the Post Office and his passengers two regular sailings each month (except in the winter). The schedule is laid out in detail in the Post Office notice below.

The Cunard Line Gets Under Way

"The only man who has dared to beat the *British Queen*," was the way they toasted Samuel Cunard when his first steamship, *Britannia*, entered Boston Harbor in 1840. By modern standards she was a small ship, midway in size between the *Great Western* and the *British Queen*. The sixty-three passengers—including Cunard himself—who made the maiden voyage, could have fit comfortably into one lifeboat of the *Queen Mary*.

But as the flagship of the first Cunard fleet, the *Britannia* marked the debut of the most enduring steamship line on the North Atlantic. She was the first to bear the famous black-topped and banded red funnel, and the first whose name bore the distinctive "-ia" ending which, until the days of the Queens, the Cunard company usually used to identify its first rank ships.

More significantly, the *Britannia*'s captain sailed with Cunard's personal instructions. "It is of the first importance to the Partners of the *Britannia*," wrote Cunard, "that she attains a Character for Speed and Safety. We trust in your vigilance of this: good steering, good look-outs, taking advantage of every slant of wind, and precautions against fire are principal elements." Henceforth, safety more than speed was to be the prime concern of every Cunard captain.

No. 2, 1840.

NOTICE TO THE PUBLIC,
AND

Instructions to all Postmasters.

MAILS for NORTH AMERICA.

GENERAL POST OFFICE,
June, 1840.

THE Packet Mails for *North America* will in future be despatched by Steam Vessels from *Liverpool* instead of Falmouth. The first Mail will be made up in London, on the **3rd July**, the Second on the **3rd August**, and after that period, (commencing with September), they will be made up in London on the **3rd and 18th** of every Month, except when either of these dates fall on the Sunday, and then on the succeeding day. The Packets will depart from Liverpool the **next Morning** as soon after the Arrival of the London Mail as possible. In the Winter Months, however, viz. *November, December, January* and *February*, but **One Mail in the Month**, that of the 3rd will be despatched.

Mails by these Packets will be made up for

BRITISH NORTH AMERICA { UPPER & LOWER CANADA, NOVA SCOTIA, NEW BRUNSWICK, PRINCE EDWARD'S ISLAND, NEWFOUNDLAND, and for the UNITED STATES;

the Postage remaining as at present, viz. an Uniform Charge of **1s.** the Single Letter, **2s.** Double, and so on, in whatever part of the United Kingdom the Letter may be posted or delivered.

Those Postmasters whose Instructions direct them to send their Letters for *Liverpool* by Cross Post, will of course forward the Correspondence intended for these Mails in the same manner.

By Command,

W. L. MABERLY.
SECRETARY.

George Burns

David MacIver

Charles MacIver

The first of the original four Cunarders, the *Britannia* (opposite) steams majestically through a lane cut in the ice that filled Boston Harbor in the frigid winter of 1844. Prominent Bostonians were so proud that the early Cunard ships called at their city, ignoring the rival port of New York, that they raised the $1,500 named in the contract (far left) for freeing the ice-bound paddlewheeler. Home port for the Cunarders for many decades was Liverpool (above), a busy shipping center on the Mersey. There, two of Cunard's hardheaded Scottish partners, David and Charles Mac-Iver, managed shipping affairs while a third, George Burns, supervised the building and fitting of their ships in Glasgow, where most of the Cunarders were constructed.

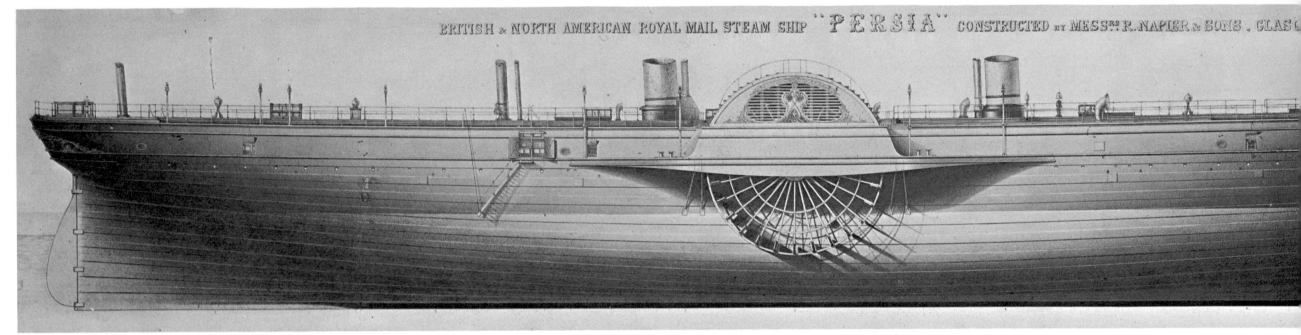

BRITISH & NORTH AMERICAN ROYAL MAIL STEAM SHIP "PERSIA" CONSTRUCTED BY MESSRS. R. NAPIER & SONS, GLASGOW

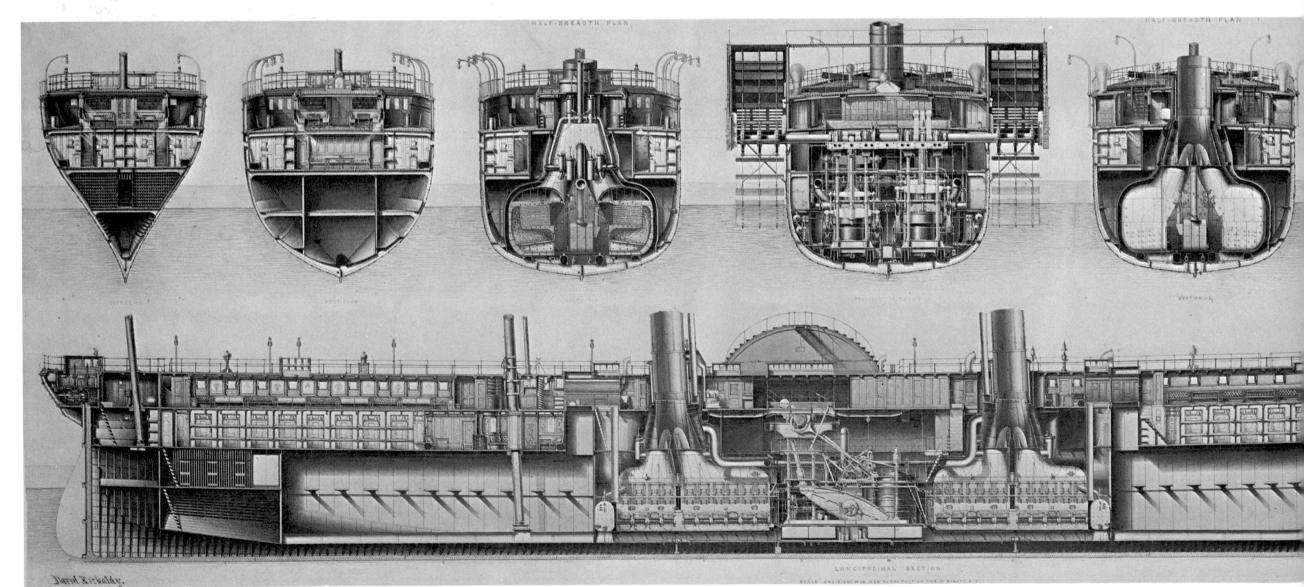

HALF-BREADTH PLAN

HALF-BREADTH PLAN

LONGITUDINAL SECTION

David Kirkaldy.

The detailed plans and cross sections of Cunard's magnificent *Persia* (left) reveal the ship's graceful lines and powerful engines. Built in 1856, Cunard's first iron-hulled ship shows the enormous strides made in steamship design in the sixteen years following the launching of the *Britannia*. The *Persia* was three times as large—3,300 tons to the *Britannia*'s 1,135 —and could carry 250 passengers, twice as many as the first Cunarder. Although economy-minded Cunard never strove for the ornate comforts provided by other lines, there were some amenities, such as the handsome china shown at right, its border decorated with representations of the original Cunard fleet. The 1862 ticket below gives the full, formal name of Cunard's line and the names of its eleven steamships that were then in service.

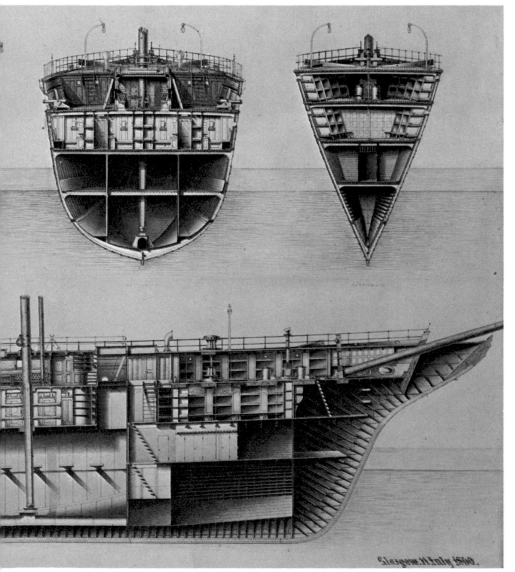

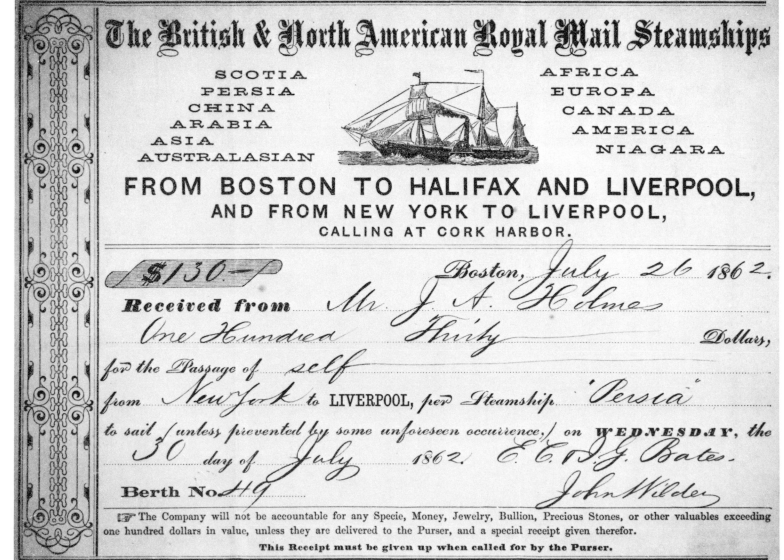

The Pleasures and Perils of Life on the Early Steamers

The steamship mania of the mid-1800s aroused an insatiable popular hunger for pictures and stories of life aboard ship. In the engraving at left, various groups of passengers promenade on the crowded deck of Cunard's *Arabia,* while others enjoy the view from the tops of paddle-boxes. The illustrations opposite appeared in an 1843 children's book, *Rollo's Tour in Europe.* Clockwise from the top are scenes of: young Rollo climbing a paddlebox; the New York wharf of the Collins Line, from which Rollo and his family made their departure; a passenger tied to the rigging by mischievous sailors; a churlish boy threatening to shoot a bird that has strayed aboard; and Rollo and his sister being shown their stateroom.

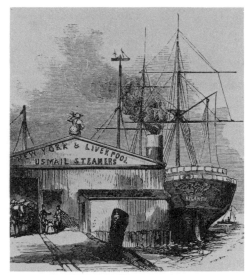

ROLLO'S TOUR IN EUROPE

ROLLO ON THE ATLANTIC

W. J. REYNOLDS & Co.
Publishers. Boston.

For the crew, life aboard was hard and often entailed dirty work. The captain worked and worried on deck and in his cabin (below, right), and the chefs were kept busy in their galleys (below, aboard a French liner) preparing five meals a day—breakfast, lunch, dinner, tea, and supper. The roughest work of all fell to the stokehole crew (opposite). Richard Henry Dana, who had served his two years before the mast, described the stokehole of the *Persia:* "In these deep and unknown regions . . . in the glare of the opening and closing furnace door, live and toil a body of grim, blackened and oily men . . . When down among them on the brick and iron floors . . . I lost all sense of being at sea."

The often violent seas of the North Atlantic could send the passengers' baggage flying about the stateroom (below) and numberless sufferers flying to the rail (below, left). Seasickness was the scourge of life aboard. One early passenger lamented that flirtation was impossible because "alas! all the young girls are sick—devilish sick." The most elaborate cure for seasickness was attempted by Henry Bessemer, inventor of the blast furnace, who in 1873 launched the Bessemer Saloon (opposite). The main cabin was suspended so that it would remain stationary while the hull rolled. But the experiment failed. The saloon rolled worse than the ship.

47

America's Pride: Gallant Bids for Supremacy on the North Atlantic

In the 1850s, Americans belatedly mounted a challenge to the near monopoly of North Atlantic steamship travel enjoyed by the British. The New York and Havre Line, the longest-lived of America's paddler companies (1850–1867), ran a small fleet on the profitable New York–Cowes–Le Havre route. Cornelius Vanderbilt, who had made his immense fortune (and earned his nickname "Commodore") running ferries in New York Harbor, built four swift ships that ran briefly from New York to Bremen as well as to English ports.

The most spectacular challenge to British supremacy was offered by Edward Knight Collins, who entered the race in 1850, with four ships and a yearly subsidy of $858,000 from the U.S. government. The Collins fleet represented a great advance both in comfort and speed, and by 1852, Collins was carrying almost twice as many passengers as Cunard. But Collins' speed records were won at a heavy cost. The strain on his vessels meant frequent and costly repairs; while the loss of two of his ships was almost certainly caused by the reckless push for speed. The losses hurt the company badly. The final blow came when the mail subsidy was cut in half. Collins went bankrupt and his last ships were sold at an auction on April Fool's Day, 1858.

The docks of New York are crammed with ships while others ply the spacious harbor in the 1852 lithograph opposite. With New York fast outstripping Boston as the gateway to America, Commodore Vanderbilt (right) and other New York magnates were prompted to enter the steamship business. Vanderbilt's first entrant in the field, which he grandiloquently styled his "yacht," was the *North Star* (below) in which he cruised European waters trying to drum up business in a dozen ports, including St. Petersburg. Vanderbilt's trip caused considerable stir, as did an account of the voyage (below, left). The *North Star* eventually joined three other Vanderbilt ships on the North Atlantic run.

THE CRUISE

OF THE

STEAM YACHT NORTH STAR;

A NARRATIVE OF THE

Excursion of Mr. Vanderbilt's Party

TO

ENGLAND, RUSSIA, DENMARK, FRANCE, SPAIN, ITALY, MALTA, TURKEY, MADEIRA, ETC.

BY THE

REV. JOHN OVERTON CHOULES, D. D.,

AUTHOR OF THE "HISTORY OF MISSIONS," "YOUNG AMERICANS ABROAD," ETC.

BOSTON:

GOULD AND LINCOLN,

59 WASHINGTON STREET.

1854.

COLLINS AND CUNARD.
RAISING THE WIND; OR, BOTH SIDES OF THE STORY.

The 1857 sailing schedule for the Collins Line (right) lists neither the *Arctic* nor the *Pacific;* both were at the bottom of the sea. But Collins, whose portrait (above, left) suggests a determined bulldog of a man, maintained a regular sailing schedule with the *Atlantic* and *Baltic,* plus a new ship, the *Adriatic,* the largest and most expensive ($1 million) wooden paddle steamer yet built. The advertisement's boast that these ships were "unequaled for elegance and comfort" seems borne out by the view of the ladies' saloon of the *Atlantic* (top), decorated with Victorian opulence. The cartoon above, from a New York weekly of 1852, shows Collins and Uncle Sam contesting a bathtub *Atlantic* with Cunard and John Bull.

THE
NEW YORK AND LIVERPOOL
UNITED STATES
MAIL STEAMERS.

THE SHIPS COMPRISING THIS LINE, ARE THE

ATLANTIC, Capt. Eldridge.   BALTIC, Capt. Comstock.   ADRIATIC, Capt. West.

These Ships having been built by contract, expressly for Government service, every care has been taken in their construction, and in their engines, to ensure strength and speed, and their accommodations for passengers are unequalled for elegance and comfort.

Price of Passage from New York to Liverpool $130, in first cabin; in second cabin, $75; from Liverpool to New York, in first cabin, 30 Guineas, and 20 Guineas, in second cabin.
An experienced Surgeon attached to each Ship.
No Berth secured until paid for.

PROPOSED DATES OF SAILING FOR 1857.

FROM NEW YORK.	FROM LIVERPOOL.
SATURDAY, January 3, 1857,	WEDNESDAY, January 7, 1857.
" " 17,	" " 21,
" " 31,	" February 4,
" February 14,	" " 18,
" March 14,	" March 4,
" April 11,	" April 1,
" May 9,	" " 26,
" " 23,	" May 29,
" June 6,	" June 10,
" " 20,	" " 24,
" July 4,	" July 8,
" " 18,	" " 22,
" August 1,	" August 5,
" " 15,	" " 19,
" September 12,	" September 2,
" " 26,	" " 30,
" October 10,	" October 14,
" " 24,	" " 28,
" November 7,	" November 11,
" " 21,	" " 25,
" December 5,	" December 9,
	" " 23,

For Freight or Passage, apply to

EDWARD K. COLLINS, 56 Wall Street, N. Y.
BROWN, SHIPLEY & Co., Liverpool.
B. G. WAINWRIGHT & Co., Paris.

Song sheets from the mid-1800s reflect the public's fascination with steamships—and with disasters. The sprightly "Sea Steamer Schottisch" (below) was illustrated with a picture of the *Baltic,* while the lugubrious ballad "The Lost Steamer" (right) laments the disappearance of Collins' *Pacific* in January, 1856. The song's cover drawing depicts the *Pacific* foundering after collision with an improbable Gothic iceberg. No one knows what really happened to the ship, which vanished with 288 people aboard; but she may well have tangled with an iceberg. Ice was a frequent peril in the North Atlantic, and Collins' captains, eager to make record-breaking crossings, often ran their ships at reckless speeds, even in poor visibility.

Filling with water from deadly gashes in its bow, Collins' *Arctic* goes down (far right) off Cape Race, the southeastern point of Newfoundland, on September 27, 1854. The *Arctic,* running fast in a fog, had collided with the small, iron-hulled, French steamer *Vesta.* At first the *Arctic*'s skipper, Captain Luce, assumed the 200-ton *Vesta,* one-fifteenth the size of his own vessel, must have sustained the greater damage, and he attempted to go to her aid. But the *Vesta*'s iron hull had watertight compartments that kept her afloat. Too late, Luce realized that his own ship, with no such bulkheads, was filling with water. There was a mad scramble for the life-boats; but some three hundred people perished and fewer than ninety survived. Among those lost were Collins' wife, daughter, and son. The hero of the tragic episode was young Stewart Holland, who kept firing the distress gun (as seen in the lithograph at right) until both he and the ship disappeared beneath the waves.

The screw propeller challenged inventors' imaginations for decades, as witness the plethora of patent designs (below). Foremost among its developers were Swedish engineer John Ericsson and England's Francis Smith. As early as 1836, Ericsson had built a small propeller-driven ship, and by 1839, Smith's *Archimedes* was steaming along at a brisk ten miles an hour. An 1845 tug-of-war (below, left), in which the propeller-driven *Rattler* pulled the paddlewheeler *Alecto* backward at two knots, was accepted as proof of the propeller's superiority—although the *Rattler* also had a stronger engine than her opponent. The *Rattler*'s builder was Isambard Kingdom Brunel, whose most daring projects garland his portrait opposite.

Sir Francis Pettit Smith

John Ericsson

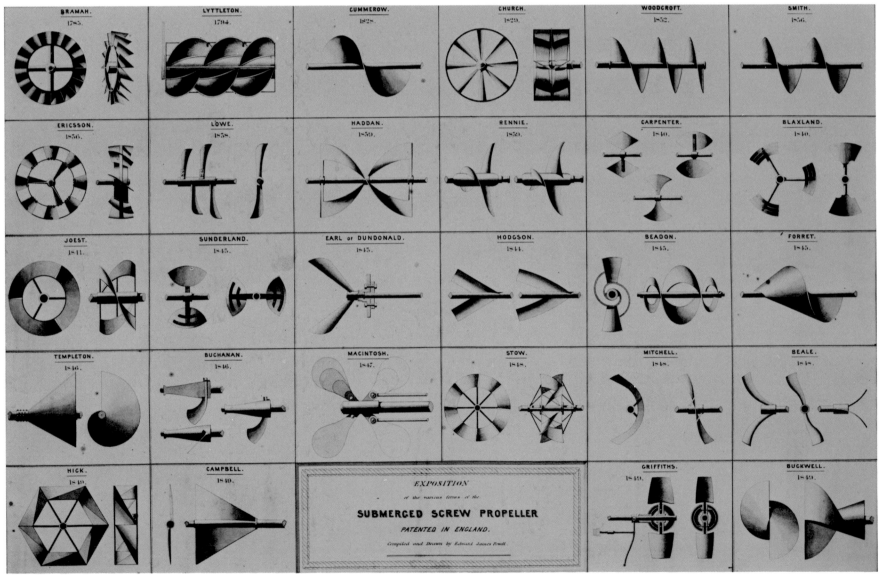

The Fathers of Invention

A ship of iron? Why, such a thing was "contrary to nature," or so said many seafaring men. But by the mid-1800s, the iron-hulled ship was becoming a reality. So was screw propulsion, another major innovation in steamship technology. The ship that decisively proved the advantages of both was the *Great Britain,* a "seagoing revolution" designed by the ubiquitous Isambard Kingdom Brunel, whose *Great Western* was still one of the fastest liners on the North Atlantic. Making her maiden voyage in July, 1845, the *Great Britain* was not only the first ocean-going steamship with an iron hull, but also the first to be fully driven by propellers.

Experiments with iron hulls began as early as the 1780s. An iron hull, it turned out, was both stronger and—curiously—more buoyant than a wooden one. Iron hulls were also free from dry rot and vermin, needed no caulking, and were less vulnerable to the dangers of fire.

The screw propeller presented marine engineers with many difficulties. For one thing, it needed a high pressure engine to operate at an effective speed; and its drive shaft required a watertight fitting in the ship's hull. But solutions were on the way: iron-hulled, screw-driven steamships would soon dominate the Atlantic.

Brunel's *Great Britain,* her 322-foot iron hull exhibiting all the grace of a clipper ship, was launched (opposite) in July, 1843, as excited crowds jammed the Bristol waterfront. The biggest and strongest ship of her day, she had six masts (one was later removed). Her massive engines (right) gave her twice the horsepower of Brunel's earlier triumph, the *Great Western.* The cross section and deck plan (below) first appeared in 1845, while the ship was being fitted out. The cross section shows the two decks of staterooms and saloons and the situation of the boilers (1), engines (2), and the shaft (15) that connected the engines to the screws. The deck plan shows the location of skylights, rigging, and stairs.

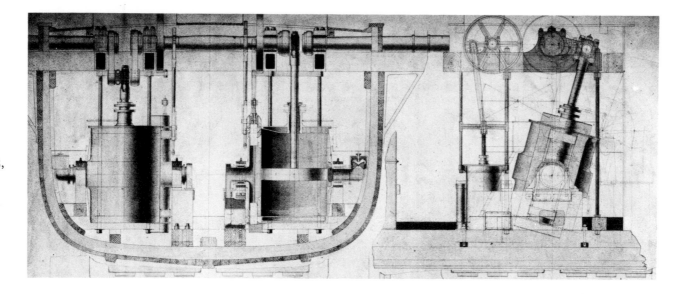

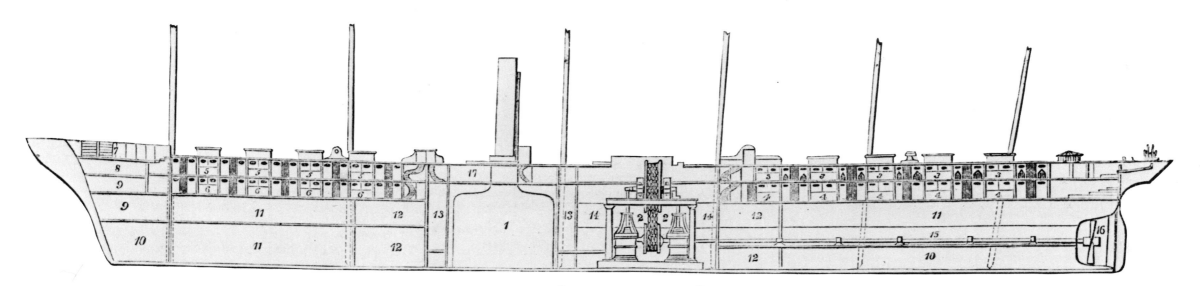

SECTION OF "THE GREAT BRITAIN."

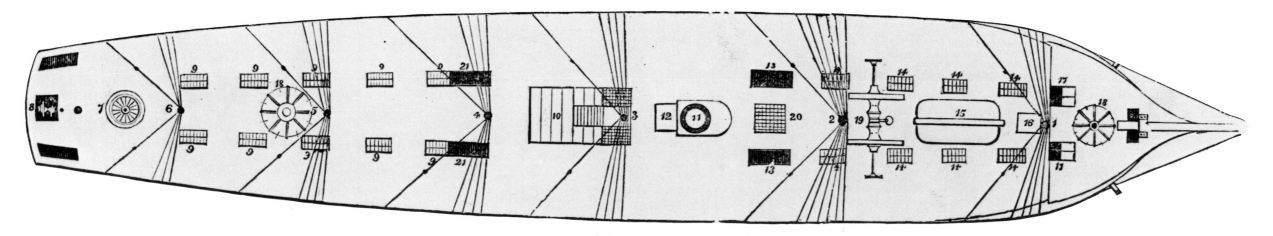

UPPER DECK OF "THE GREAT BRITAIN."

The *Great Britain* had a long, tumultuous life. After several runs to New York, she ran aground in Dundrum Bay on the Irish coast (left). Beached for eleven months, her iron hull easily withstood winter gales that would have made matchsticks of a wooden-hulled ship. Refloated and her interior fittings repaired, she was put on the Australian run, making thirty-two round trips to Melbourne. Converted into a grain ship in 1881, she sailed for another few years until beached in the Falkland Islands. There she lay until 1970 when her historic hull, still largely intact, was put aboard a submersible pontoon (below) and she was towed 8,000 miles back to her birthplace, Bristol, there to be converted into a marine museum.

The gigantic hull of the *Great Eastern* takes shape in 1857 (below), her fifty-eight-foot height dwarfing nearby riverside dwellings. Built on a muddy section of the Thames' bank called the Isle of Dogs, she had to be launched sideways because the river was too narrow to receive her 680-foot length. Great iron chains, each link weighing seventy pounds, were readied to check the ship should she slide into the river too swiftly. As it turned out, it took three months to inch the hull into the Thames. The extended launch bankrupt the company that built her and was a severe strain on Brunel, who oversaw the entire operation. The "Little Giant," wearing his usual high beaver hat, is seen (right) standing beside a drum of launch chain.

Brunel's Mighty Vision Begets the First Giant Steamer

Brunel was small in stature, but his ambition and self-confidence were gigantic. Not content with having built 25 railroads, 125 railroad bridges, 5 pioneering suspension spans, and a complete prefabricated hospital for Crimean War wounded, not to mention the *Great Western* and *Great Britain,* the audacious engineer designed the *Great Eastern,* five times the size of the largest vessel then afloat. Longer than two football fields, she had two engines, one for the fifty-eight-foot paddle wheels and the other for the twenty-four-foot propeller.

Brunel intended the *Great Eastern* to virtually monopolize British trade and passenger service to the Far East, carrying six thousand tons of goods and three thousand passengers; her immense size would enable her to carry enough coal for the entire ten thousand mile trip. But the ship's $5 million cost bankrupted the builders and her new owners put her on the Atlantic run. Failing to make a profit, they opened her to sightseers.

The great ship finally came into her own in 1866, when she laid the first successful telegraph cable under the Atlantic. But she ended her days as an amusement center plastered with advertisements. A ship fifty years ahead of her time, she was not exceeded in size until the *Lusitania* was launched in 1906.

1 These rare photographs show: the *Great Eastern*'s flank being sheathed in steel plates;

2 the towering bulkheads that divided the ship into twelve watertight compartments;

5 stockholders inspecting the ship's partially completed, 692-foot-long main deck;

6 builder John Scott Russell, beneath the frame of a partially completed paddlewheel box;

3 a view of the sharp bow showing the narrowness of the streamlined hull;

4 sheathing being completed on the stern, as seen from the Thames-side;

7 the port paddle wheel and (foreground) an enormous drum of launching chain;

8 a bow view of the *Great Eastern* ready for launching in November, 1857.

THE GREAT EASTERN.

25,000 tons Burthen.
Length, 692 feet.
Breadth, 83 „
Depth, 58 „
Across Paddle Boxes, 144 feet.
4 Decks, 10 Boilers.
112 Furnaces, and 10 Anchors.
Combined Steam Power, 3,000 horses.

Draft of Water . . . . 30 feet.
    when Laden . . 34 „
Spreads 6,500 Square yards of Canvass.
Weight of Cable . . . . 5,000 tons.
Coals . . . . 8,500 „
Water Tanks, Machinery, &c. . . 8,500 „
The Cable was submerged in 3 Tanks, each 59 feet in
    diameter and 20 feet deep.

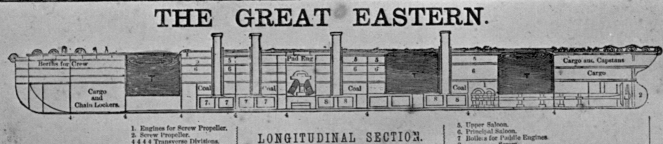

1. Engines for Screw Propeller.
2. Screw Propeller.
4 4 4 4 Transverse Divisions.
T Tanks containing the Cable.

5. Upper Saloon.
6. Principal Saloon.
7 Boilers for Paddle Engines.
8. „ „ Screw „

LONGITUDINAL SECTION.

THE NEW ATLANTIC CABLE.

CONDUCTOR.—A Copper Strand, consisting of seven wires, weighing 300 lbs. per nautical mile, embedded for solidity in Gutta Percha and Stockholm Tar, termed "Chatterton's Compound."

INSULATION.—(A.) Four layers of Gutta Percha, laid on alternately with four thin layers of Chatterton's Compound. Weight 400 lbs. per mile. The Copper Strand and this insulation form the "core;" about half an inch in diameter.

EXTERNAL PROTECTION.—(C.) Ten solid wires, each wire is surrounded separately with five Strands of Manilla Yarn (B,) and the whole laid spirally round the core, which is padded with ordinary hemp. This hemp and the yarn being saturated with a preservative mixture.

THE SHORE END, in addition to the above, is wrapped with yarn (D) which is then covered by twelve strands of iron-wire, each strand being composed of three galvanised iron-wires (E,) each of which is nearly a quarter inch in diameter. The weight of the completed Shore Cable is 20 tons to the mile. The diameter of the shore end is 2½ inches. At its junction with the main cable, it gradually tapers through a space of 500 yards to the size of the latter.

DEEPEST WATER ENCOUNTERED, 2,400 fathoms, or less than 2½ nautical miles.
LENGTH OF CABLE SHIPPED ON BOARD THE GREAT EASTERN, 2,300 miles.
DISTANCE FROM IRELAND TO NEWFOUNDLAND, 1,670 nautical miles.

THE OLD ATLANTIC CABLE

CONDUCTOR.—A copper strand, consisting of 7 wires, weight 107 lbs. per mile.
INSULATION.—Gutta Percha, laid on in 3 coverings, weighing 261 lbs. per mile.
LENGTH OF CABLE SHIPPED in 1858, 2,174 nautical miles.

EXTERNAL PROTECTION.—Eighteen strands of Charcoal Iron-wire, each strand composed of seven wires, laid spirally round the core, which latter was previously padded with a serving of hemp, saturated with a tar mixture.

Cable of 1858; exact size.

Cable of 1865; exact size.

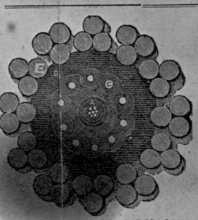

Section of Shore end Atlantic Cable of 1865;
exact size. Valentia end 27 miles; Newfoundland end 3 miles.

Section of Cable, 1858; exact size.

Section of Cable of 1865; exact size.

Watching the *Great Eastern* start her trials
in September, 1859, Brunel (second from
right in the photo above, right) and John
Scott Russell, the ship's builder (far left),
stand on a dock at Thames-side. Only hours
after this photograph was taken Brunel,
exhausted by the effort of building and
launching his leviathan, died of a stroke at
age fifty-three. The nobility of the ship
that Brunel and Russell had wrought is
captured in the contemporary lithograph
opposite, showing the *Great Eastern* under
power of propeller, paddle wheels, and sail;
the circles at the bottom of the painting
represent cross sections of the transatlantic
telegraph cable laid by the *Great Eastern*.
Above is a photograph showing a view of
the ship's ornate Victorian interior.

The *Great Eastern* lies serenely in the tiny port of Heart's Content, Newfoundland (left), after laying the transatlantic telegraph cable in 1866. The ship later carried the longest cable ever laid—2,584 nautical miles—across the Indian Ocean from Bombay to Aden. The cables, coiled in the hold, were paid out through gears in the stern. In the engraving below, electricians examine the cable after a break. Never a money-maker as a passenger ship, the *Great Eastern* did attract thousands of sightseers. Put on show as a curiosity in New York, she drew such hordes that railroads ran special excursions (right). Her pathetic end, as a floating billboard and amusement hall, was caricatured in the cartoon reproduced on the opposite page.

GREAT EASTERN EXCURSION.

The undersigned has completed arrangements to run a series of

EXCURSION TRAINS

—— OVER THE ——

Passumpsic, Sullivan, Vermont Valley, VERMONT & MASSACHUSETTS, ASHUELOT, Connecticut River,

AND

NEW HAVEN, HARTFORD & SPRINGFIELD RAILROADS,

AND WITH THE

SPLENDID STEAMER ELM CITY,

FROM NEW HAVEN, TO

NEW YORK,

DURING THE STAY IN THAT CITY OF THE

GREAT EASTERN,

AT ONE HALF THE USUAL FARES.

THE FIRST EXCURSION TRAIN

Will leave Barton, at 8.00 A. M., MONDAY, July 9th, 1860; White River Junction, 12.40, P. M.; Bellows Falls, 2.40 P. M.; Brattleboro, 3.35 P. M.; Keene, 2.10 P. M.; Springfield, by Extra Train at 7.00, P. M.

RETURNING:

LEAVE NEW YORK, FROM PECK SLIP, ON WEDNESDAY, AT 11.00 P. M., Arriving in Springfield in time to connect with the 7.45 A. M., Train for the North, by which excursionists will reach Barton, and Intermediate Stations, the same day. This arrangement will give the passengers **TWO DAYS IN NEW YORK TO VISIT THE GREAT EASTERN,** and other objects of interest in the City.

SAMUEL A. COOLEY.

EARLY NOTICE WILL BE GIVEN OF THE SECOND EXCURSION TRAIN.

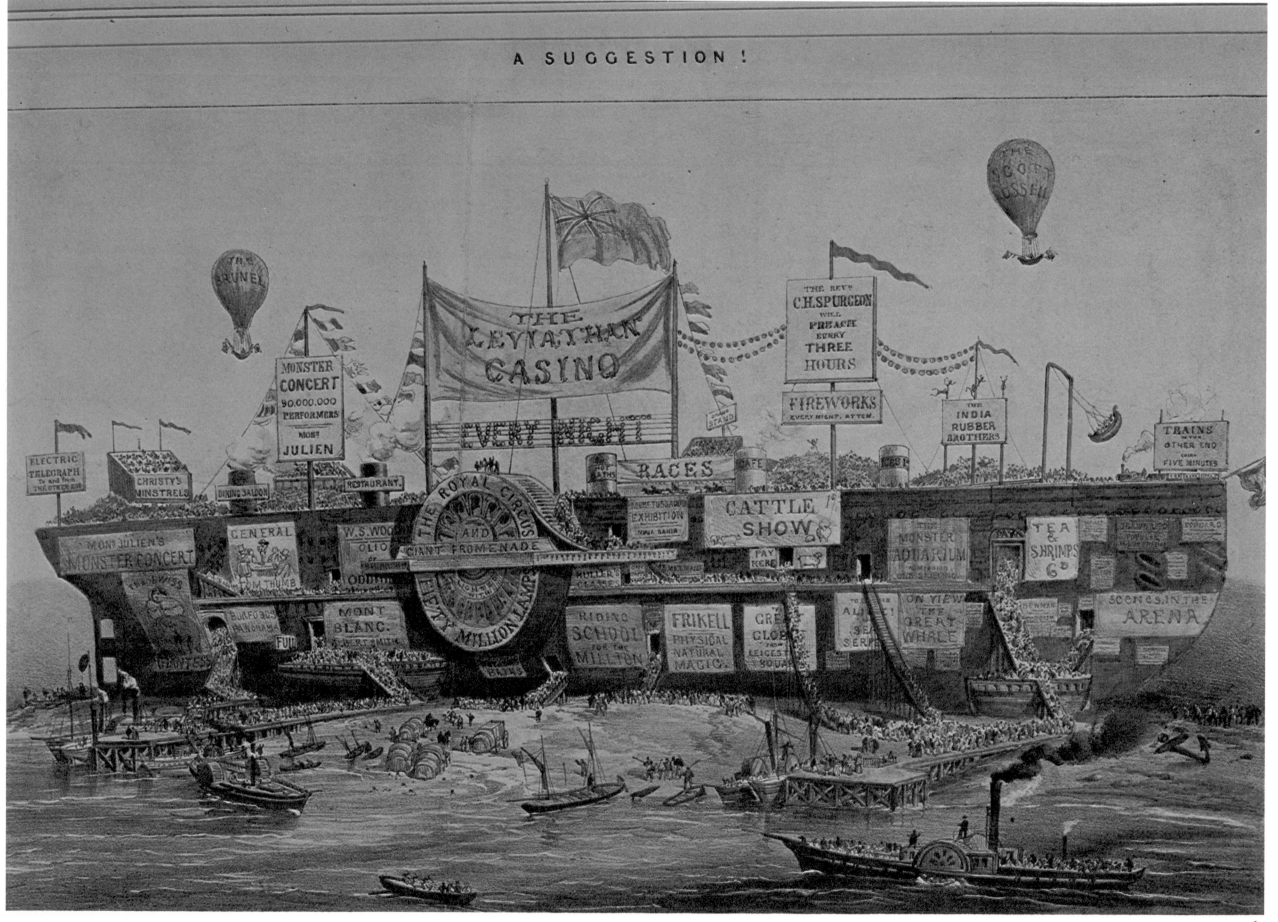

The Emigrant Experience

1850–1914

Driven by hunger and oppression, waves of emigrants arrive on Europe's shores seeking passage to America. . . . Hundreds are jammed into suffocating holds; disease devastates entire ships. . . . As the number of emigrants steadily rises, steam replaces sail . . . new steamship lines appear to meet the need . . . and conditions improve. The journey is cut from forty days to fourteen . . . and by the early 1900s, some ships are even providing cooks and stewards in steerage. . . . Meanwhile, the number of emigrants grows to a million every year, enabling shipowners to keep the luxury liners afloat . . . and a nation growing.

Apprehensive but resolute, a young couple takes a backward glance toward their homeland in Ford Madox Brown's sentimental painting, *The Last of England* (left), executed in the 1850s. In reality, the hundreds of thousands of Europeans who set sail for the New World in the nineteenth century left with few regrets. Even the experience of traveling in such crowded conditions as those found aboard the Red Star Line's *Pennland*, pictured below on an Antwerp to New York run in 1893, were not enough to dissuade them. Turn-of-the-century immigrants were required to carry some proof of good health, such as the Inspection Card shown at bottom, which accompanied a Russian immigrant arriving in 1917.

America held out to Europeans the dream
of prosperity. As caricatured in the
American cartoon (left), it was impossible
for John Bull to hold back the fleeing
English. The Germans were no more
successful in keeping venturesome
members of the populace at home, no
matter how awful the emigrant ships may
have been. An 1847 German cartoon
(opposite, left) compares, quite rightly,
the shipowners to herring packers.
Neither cartoon was likely to reach as
many people as the two announcements
opposite. *Direkte till Amerika* promises
direct passage from Göteborg, Sweden, to
Chicago aboard ships of the Anchor Line.
The land offering describes opportunities
in western New York.

They came to America by the millions: the greatest
mass movement of people the world had ever seen.

From Ireland, Great Britain, and Germany they
came; from Norway and Sweden; from Italy, Austria–
Hungary, Russia, Poland, Estonia, and Lithuania;
from Greece, Albania, Serbia, Bulgaria, Syria, and
Armenia: thirty-five million people in the century
preceding 1920.

And it was the steamship that made such numbers
possible, carrying in later years upwards of a
thousand emigrants with each crossing: a million
every year during the peak years from 1900 to
1914. Thus, the steamship played a crucial role in
shaping the character of America.

Uprooted by famine, poverty, epidemics, and
revolution, the emigrants trekked from their wasted
farms, villages, and from the factory towns. They
came mostly on foot, but also by cart or riverboat, and
later by train if they could afford it. They came
because they had no alternative. Although to journey
meant to risk everything, at home there was no
work, no food, and no hope. In America, they had
heard, there were jobs and free land.

So they came to the shores of Europe, to the
growing seaport towns. At first, in the packet ship
days, it mattered little which port an emigrant

chose. Sailings on the cheap emigrant ships were
infrequent and irregular. The prospective passenger
dickered with the captain for his fare, then spent what
money he had keeping body and soul together for
the days or weeks it took for the ship to be cargoed up.

But by the mid-1800s, bookings were being
handled by shipping agents. The bigger companies
had taken over the operations of smaller shipowners,
and there were regularly scheduled sailings, announced in distant villages by placards tacked to
doorposts and gateways. Emigrant traffic funneled
more and more through a few main ports: Queenstown in Ireland, Liverpool in England, and, on the
Continent, Bremen, Hamburg, Le Havre, Antwerp,
and later, Naples, Genoa, and Trieste.

Having survived the overland journey and the
miserable penny-a-night lodgings that introduced
him to urban life, the emigrant boarded the ship
that was to be, depending on his luck and stamina,
either his coffin or his ferry to a new life. Few looked
back. As one Queenstown captain reported: "They
all seemed glad to leave their native land. We
hardly got outside the harbor before fiddles and
concertinas would be produced, and they would be
dancing away on the foredeck."

But the joy was short-lived. Ahead lay the broad

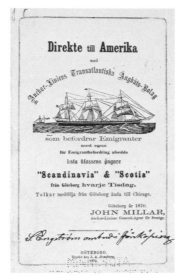

Atlantic: three thousand miles of sea to cross, a universe of water. For most, the journey was a nightmare. In the early days, emigrants were often transported in former slave ships. And like the slaves before them, they were packed into the suffocating holds like so many head of cattle: six to ten people in bunks ten feet wide, five feet long, and three feet high. "Between decks," wrote one historian, "was like a loathsome dungeon. When the hatchways were opened under which the people were stowed, the steam rose, and the stench was like that from a pen of pigs."

Here the emigrants lived for forty days—or for two or three months if the winds and tides were against them. Disease was rampant: cholera, dysentery, yellow fever, smallpox, and "ship fever," or typhus. On many voyages ten percent or more of the steerage passengers died at sea.

Conditions later improved substantially aboard the emigrant steamers. In 1850, a young Englishman, William Inman, became the first to offer cheap steamship passage to emigrants. (Until then, steamships had carried mostly first-class passengers and express cargo.) Inman was also the first to send emigrant ships to Queenstown, thereby sparing the Irish an expensive and miserable journey across the

Irish Sea to Liverpool. For £6 (or $30), Inman not only transported the emigrant to America but fed him three meals a day and provided towels and soap.

Once Inman eased the way for emigrants, other companies followed suit. In fact, during the latter half of the century, it was emigrant fares that kept most shipping lines afloat—although the emphasis in steamship advertisements was on the first-class amenities of speed, luxury, and comfort.

The steamship reduced the emigrant's time at sea to two weeks, and later to just over one week. But the crossing was still no picnic. Steerage quarters were crowded and noisy and there was a minimum of privacy. The poor slept on bare canvas bunks, eighteen inches wide and six feet long, while those that could afford it bought straw mattresses that were thrown overboard when the ship entered New York. Most shocking of all was the fact that as late as 1890, it was common practice for shipowners to transport live cattle on the trip from America to Europe in the same space that was to be occupied by human cargo on the return journey.

For the emigrants, however, the journey, no matter how appalling and terrifying, seemed worth the effort. And for those that survived, arrival meant the promise of a new beginning.

The revolutionary spirit in Germany brought Berliners to the barricades in 1848 (opposite), and many Germans to the conviction that their future in the fatherland was shaky at best. Between 1846 and 1855, more than a million of them emigrated to America, beginning their slow journeys by such means as the Rhine vessel (below), which carried them to one of the transatlantic ports. At about the same time, the steady flow of dislocated Irish swelled to a mass movement following the Great Potato Famine of 1846, and farewell scenes like that at right became commonplace. Even some English (bottom right), suffering population pressures and industrial turmoil, pulled up roots to find passage westward to a better life.

A Steamship Armada to Ferry the Multitude

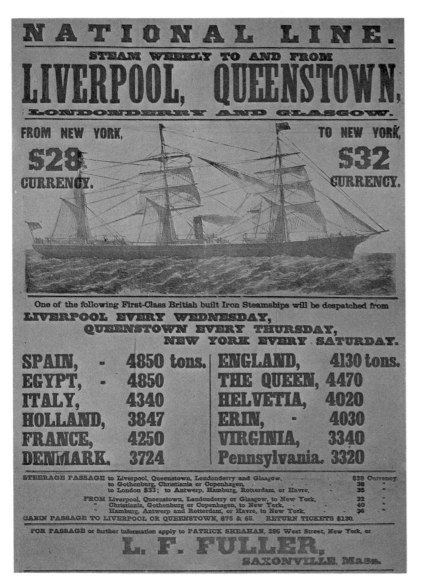

"Emigration made easy," read the handbills that William Inman distributed throughout the hungry villages of Ireland: "Three thousand miles at a half-penny a mile." The lure worked. By charging low fares and providing fast and reasonably comfortable passage to America aboard his iron-hulled steamships—beginning with the *City of Glasgow* in 1850—Inman succeeded in capturing fully one-third of all passenger traffic across the Atlantic. And he did it without the benefit of a government subsidy.

Other companies—including Cunard—clamored to cash in on this new mother lode of revenue. By the peak year of 1873, when almost half a million emigrants arrived in America, there were seventeen lines operating a total of 173 ships between Europe and New York. German emigrants alone were crossing in such numbers that North German Lloyd, a company founded in 1856 from a coalition of small steamboat lines, was running two and sometimes three ships to America every week.

Meanwhile, competition among the lines made the emigrant's crossing cheaper—if no less tedious. In the mid-1860s, Cunard's steerage fare was fixed as low as £3 15s. (about $18), including "a full dietary." And there were times when an emigrant could get across the ocean for as little as $12.

The American Civil War all but drove United States ships out of the immigration business in the 1860s, and British and French interests seized the opportunity to inaugurate several new transatlantic lines, including the National. By 1870 National was handling twice as many emigrant passages as Cunard, but poor management and the granting of mail subsidies to competitors eventually reversed the tide; National dropped out of the passenger business in 1892. The Allan Line began service in 1854, and soon made a name as the chief transporter of emigrants to Quebec, with twice-weekly crossings.

No. 42275
INMAN LINE.

ERNEST S. INMAN,
General Manager,
22, WATER STREET, LIVERPOOL.

C. & W. D. SEYMOUR & CO.
Agents,
QUEENSTOWN.

INMAN STEAMSHIP CO.
LIMITED,
1, BROADWAY, NEW YORK.

EIVES & ALLEN,
Agents,
99, CANNON ST., LONDON, E.C.

PASSENGERS' CONTRACT TICKET.

1.—A Contract Ticket in this Form must be given to every Passenger engaging a Passage from the United Kingdom to any place out of Europe, and not being within the Mediterranean sea, immediately on the payment or deposit by such Passenger of the whole or any part of the passage money, for, or in respect of the passage engaged.

2.—The Victualling Scale for the voyage must be printed in the Body of the Ticket.

3.—All the Blanks must be correctly filled in, and the Ticket must be legibly signed with the Christian names and Surnames, and Address of the party issuing the same.
4.—The Day and the Month on which the Passengers are to embark must be inserted in words and not in Figures.
5.—When once issued, this Ticket must not be withdrawn from the Passenger, nor any alteration, addition, or erasure made in it.

Steam-ship **CITY OF**_____ (Or other of Company's Steamers,) of _____ tons register, to take in Passengers at **LIVERPOOL** via Queenstown for **NEW YORK** on the _____ day of _____ 188__

NAMES.	AGES.	EQUAL TO STATUTE ADULTS.

I engage that the Persons named in the margin hereof shall be provided with a Steerage Passage to, and shall be landed at the port of **NEW YORK**, in the United States of America, in the Steam-ship City of_____ (or other of Company's Steamers,) with not less than ten cubic feet for Luggage for each Statute Adult, and shall be victualled during the voyage and the time of detention at any place before its termination, according to the subjoined scale, for the sum of £_____ including Government Dues before Embarkation, and Head Money, if any, at the place of landing, and every other charge, except freight for excess of luggage beyond the quantity above specified, and I hereby acknowledge to have received the sum of £_____ in _____ payment.

The following quantities, at least, of Water and Provisions (to be issued daily) will be supplied by the Master of the Ship as required by Law, viz.:—To each Statute adult 3 quarts of Water daily, exclusive of what is necessary for cooking the articles required by the Passengers' Act to be issued in a cooked state; and a weekly allowance of Provisions according to the following scale:—3½lbs. of Bread, 1½ lbs. Fresh Bread, 1lb. Flour, 1½ lbs. Oatmeal, 1½lbs. Potatoes, 1½lbs. Peas, 4oz. Raisins, 2lbs. Beef, 1½lbs. Pork, 1lb. Fish, 2oz. Tea, 2oz. Coffee or Cocoa, 1lb. Sugar, 1 Gill Molasses, 1 Gill Vinegar, 3oz. Salt, 1oz. Mustard and Pepper, Which will be cooked by the Servants of the Company, and served out according to the following

BILL OF FARE.
Breakfast at 8 o'clock, Dinner at 1 o'clock, Supper at 6 o'clock.

SUNDAY.—*Breakfast,* Coffee, Sugar and Fresh Bread. *Dinner,* Beef and Potatoes, Flour Pudding, with Raisins and Molasses *Supper,* Tea, Sugar and Biscuit.
MONDAY.—*Breakfast,* Oatmeal Porridge and Molasses. *Dinner,* Pea Soup, Pork and Bread. *Supper,* Tea, Sugar and Biscuit.
TUESDAY.—*Breakfast,* Coffee, Sugar and Fresh Bread. *Dinner,* Fish and Potatoes. *Supper,* Tea, Sugar and Biscuit.
WEDNESDAY.—*Breakfast,* Oatmeal Porridge and Molasses. *Dinner,* Pea Soup, Beef and Rice. *Supper,* Tea, Sugar and Biscuit.
THURSDAY.—*Breakfast,* Coffee, Sugar and Fresh Bread. *Dinner,* Pea Soup, Pork and Potatoes. *Supper,* Tea, Sugar and Biscuit.
FRIDAY.—*Breakfast,* Coffee, Sugar and Fresh Bread. *Dinner,* Fish and Potatoes. *Supper,* Tea, Sugar and Biscuit.

SATURDAY.—*Breakfast,* Oatmeal Porridge and Molasses. *Dinner,* Pea Soup, Beef and Rice.

¼lb. of Beef or Pork will be substituted for 1½lb. Oatmeal.
1lb. of Flour will be substituted for 1lb. Rice or Split Peas.
½oz. of Coffee will be substituted for 2oz. Tea.
½lb. of Molasses do.

Coffee or Cocoa, with Sugar and Fresh Bread, may be substituted for Porridge and Molasses on Monday, Wednesday and Saturday Mornings. Children under 10 years of age receive half the above. As the Provisions will be cooked and served out in rations, each Passenger will be required to provide a Tin Plate, Quart Mug, Knife, Fork, Spoon, and Water Can, also Bedding.

NOTICE TO PASSENGERS.

1.—If Passengers, through no default of their own, are not received on board on the day named in their Contract Tickets, or fail to obtain a Passage in the Ship, they should apply to the Government Emigration Officer at the Port, who will assist them in obtaining redress under the Passengers' Act.
2.—Passengers should carefully keep this part of their Contract Ticket till after the end of the voyage.

N.B.—THIS CONTRACT TICKET IS EXEMPT FROM STAMP DUTY.

☞ This Ticket is issued subject to the following conditions:—That it is available only for the date for which it is issued. If not used for that date, or is lost or mislaid, it is cancelled, and the Passage Money absolutely forfeited; and that Passenger's Luggage is carried only upon the following conditions:—
The Company carries Passenger's Luggage and Goods for which a Bill of Lading is not signed, subject to the express stipulation:—That it is not to be liable for the loss of, or injury to, any Article or Articles, or Property, of the descriptions mentioned in the Schedule hereto, contained in any Parcel or Package, when the value of such Article or Articles, or Property, shall exceed the sum of £10 unless at the time of the delivery thereof to the Company the value thereof shall have been declared by the person or persons sending or delivering the same, and the increased charge also mentioned in the said Schedule, or an engagement to pay the same, be accepted by the Company or unless the loss or injury occur by the wilful act of the Company or its Servants. And that, in respect of all such Luggage or Goods as above-mentioned and of whatever value, the Company is not to be liable for any risk except in the forms of Bill of Lading used by the Company.

SCHEDULE.—ARTICLES.—Gold or Silver Manufactured or Unmanufactured, or in Shape of Coin, Plated Articles, Glass, China, Jewellery, Precious Stones, Trinkets, Watches, Clocks, Time-Pieces, Mosaics, Bills, Bank Notes of any Country, Orders, Notes or Securities for payment of Money, Stamps, Maps, Writings, Title Deeds, Paintings, Engravings, Pictures, Silks, Furs, Lace, Cashmere, Manufactured or Unmanufactured, made up into Clothes, or otherwise. } **RATE OF CHARGE**—One per cent. on declared value.

Not including American Railway Fare. { Deposit £_____ Balance £_____ Total £_____ } { To be paid at the Office at the Port of Embarkation one day before the above date for sailing.

Signature _____

On behalf of ERNEST STOBART INMAN,

LIVERPOOL, _____ 188

William Inman, portrayed above, stands out as the great innovator in nineteenth century transatlantic travel and the first man to grasp the tremendous potential of "screw motive power." His iron-hulled *City of Glasgow,* put into regular Liverpool-to-Philadelphia service in 1850, proved that steerage passengers could be transported at a cost competitive with the much slower sailing packets. Among his innovations were cooked meals in steerage, as set forth in the detailed contract at left. Inman was also the first to cater particularly to the Irish, making Queenstown (above), later renamed Cobh, a major port of call.

The French were late arrivals in the steamship trade, establishing the Compagnie Générale Transatlantique, the French Line, only in 1864, with the commissioning of the two Clyde-built ships, the *Washington* (left) and the slightly faster *Lafayette* (below). Both vessels were designed as ocean paddlers with the emphasis on speed; but even before they were launched developments in screw propulsion by rival English companies proved that the traditional paddle wheel system was outmoded. Within four years both ships were converted and enlarged. Because the original engines were designed to drive two paddle wheels, the conversions were to twin screws, the first used in transatlantic service.

Launching the French Line's "Belle Epoque"

After both Cherbourg and Brest had been tried and rejected as home ports, the Compagnie Générale Transatlantique chose Le Havre, pictured (below, right), which was closer to Paris. The brothers Emile and Isaac Pereire (bottom right), were the chief organizers of the line. Already rich from speculations in other transportation ventures, they won from the government the promise of an annual subsidy. French emigration never reached the level of other countries, but French Line agents in Germany and elsewhere did such a job of selling steerage space that Le Havre's dockside was regularly crowded with eager clients. In the 1886 engraving below, passengers are shown leaving the boat train and boarding a French liner.

A Hard Passage to a New Life

Purchasing a ticket, as shown in the engraving (opposite, left) of a ticket agent's office, was only the first of many hurdles a prospective traveler had to clear but it was a major one. Before the various governments began to intervene, it was not uncommon for an inexperienced country fellow to buy his ticket from some broker only to discover, when he reached dockside (opposite, lower right), that he had been swindled and that the ship did not exist or the ticket was invalid. Even when no fraud was involved, he often had to endure a long wait in a barracks-like boardinghouse (opposite, right), until space became available and the shipping company had loaded a sufficient amount of cargo to make the journey profitable.

Finally, the long-awaited day arrived. Gathering up mattresses, blankets, a few precious belongings, and such extra provisions as seemed likely to make the passage bearable, emigrants prepared to board in dockside scenes like that at right. While top-hatted first-class passengers could take their time saying good-bye, those ticketed in steerage were well-advised to arrive early to get the best bunk. But even the best was seldom better than cargo space, barely swept clean of the cattle, cotton, or other freight that had gone to Europe on the eastbound run.

Sails drawing and steam up, another
crowded emigrant ship leaves home (opposite). Often whole communities, their
spiritual leaders included, traveled together.
Religious life went on at sea much as it
had on land; above left, one such group
gathers on deck to hear their pastor deliver
a sermon. Dining customs did not fare so
well; the highly romanticized 1849 engraving above shows some of the passengers preparing a communal stew but
immigrant memoirs have left a more lurid
picture of the period, which predated
company-provided meals. One voyager
found his seaborne lodgings "filled with
every sort of filth, broken biscuit, bones,
rags, and refuse of every description,
putrefying and filled with maggots."

Cramped berths, like those at right, roughly ten feet wide by five feet long and just high enough to permit occupants to sit up, often accommodated one or more families in the early days of sailing packets. But by mid-century, governments on both sides of the Atlantic were beginning to exercise some control over living conditions. The model for such statutes was the British Passengers' Act, put into force in 1855, soon after William Inman had voluntarily introduced a number of improvements. Steerage then began to come closer to the scene above, where adequate light, air, privacy—and even a broom—are provided, and there is room enough for one family to spread out a map on which to plan their journey once ashore.

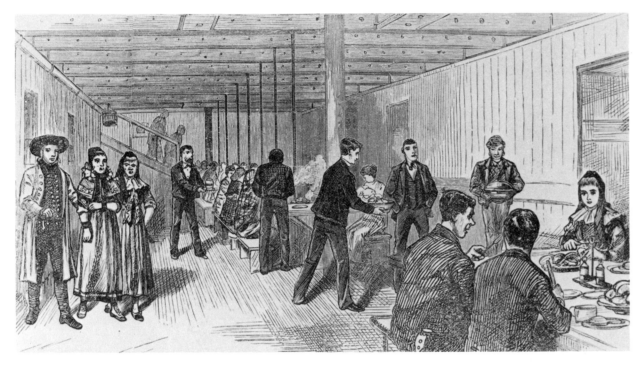

Inman's *City of Brussels,* the first ship to cross the Atlantic in less than eight days, was also the leader in steerage comforts, as the steward-attended dining hall (above) indicates. Inman's mark was clearly the one to beat when countryman Thomas Ismay, portrayed at top, launched the White Star Line in 1871. By dint of partnership with the innovative Belfast shipyard of Harland & Wolff, White Star's very first steamers, the *Oceanic, Atlantic,* and *Baltic,* trimmed time from the *Brussels* and offered steerage accommodations on a par with Inman's and at bargain rates. The prospectus reproduced at right, which was principally directed to Americans traveling eastward, offered free passage for Europe-bound babies.

No. 89.

WHITE STAR LINE.

PROPOSED SAILINGS OF WHITE STAR STEAMERS.
CARRYING THE U. S. MAILS.
FROM COMPANY'S WHARF, PIER 52 N. R., NEW YORK,
FOR LIVERPOOL, CALLING AT QUEENSTOWN.

To Land Passengers and Mails as follows:

CELTIC, Saturday, 23d Jan. 7 A.M.	**BALTIC**,	Sat., 13th Feb.	11 A.M.
OCEANIC, " 30th " 11 A.M.	**ADRIATIC**,	" 20th "	3 P.M.
REPUBLIC, " 6th Feb. 3 P.M.	**CELTIC**,	" 27th "	10 A.M.

When issuing outward tickets be careful to insert the name of Steamer and date of sailing, also giving the departure one hour earlier than above. This is important, as it will prevent passengers reaching the city too late to embark.

Passengers requiring bedding, eating and drinking utensils for the voyage, can purchase them at the wharf for $3.50 full set, any extra article necessary will be furnished at reasonable prices.

Yours truly,

ALFRED LAGERGREN,
Western Agent.

Chicago, Jan. 21st, 1875.

STEERAGE PASSAGE TO AND FROM

Liverpool and Queenstown,	$20
Glasgow, Derry, Belfast, Dublin,	21
London, Cardiff, Bristol,	23
Hamburg, Havre, Antwerp, Rotterdam, Amsterdam, Harlingen,	24
Gothenburg, Christiania, Copenhagen, Bremen, Paris, Manheim,	27

Children under 12 years of age, half price. Infants under 1 year $3 to New York; free from New York.

At One Journey's End, a New Journey's Beginning

In 1855, the authorities in New York began to intercept the hoards of ship-weary immigrants before they reached shore, going out to the Narrows to meet arriving ships in order to sort out the sick and potentially infectious for delivery to a special hospital; the rest were transferred to barges (below, left) for orderly processing at facilities on the southern tip of Manhattan Island. A receiving station was set up in Castle Garden, a former theater (below), and there immigrants supposedly could find helpful information to send them on their way. In practice, however, Castle Garden was an ideal gathering place for every manner of swindler with a clever scheme for separating the immigrant from his money.

New York was, for most, only a transfer point to some still far-off destination, and agents serving a vast network of private rail, coach, and riverboat transit systems congregated in and around Castle Garden selling tickets. The Hudson River barge that is shown in the illustration at left ran from Castle Garden to the Erie Railroad depot and, as the large letters on its deckhouse advertise, it offered anyone with the price of a railway ticket connections all the way to San Francisco. The harrowing experiences of the newcomers were favorite subjects for songwriters. "Only an Immigrant"—a heartrending ballad which was published in 1879—warned that predators were waiting to prey upon the unwary.

The New Emigration: A Million a Year Westward Bound

The flood tide of emigration to America reached the highwater mark in the years between the turn of the century and the start of World War I. During that time, some thirteen million people were admitted to the United States. They came in such numbers that by 1914, one-third of the population of the country was foreign born.

It was no coincidence that 1907, the year in which the number of emigrants admitted to the United States reached an all time high of 1,285,349, was also the year when Cunard's *Mauretania* and *Lusitania* made their maiden voyages. These giants, along with the other superliners of the era, were designed specifically to meet the huge demand for cheap, safe passage to America. Each of the two Cunard ships could carry 1,180 third-class passengers with each crossing, while fully half of the 3,500 berths aboard Hamburg–America's *Imperator* were reserved for steerage passengers.

The new emigrants—those who journeyed to America after 1880—came mostly from eastern and southern Europe: from Austria–Hungary, Italy, and Russia. Like their predecessors, they were regarded as a race apart—as not only poorer than first- and second-class passengers but also morally inferior. The chasm separating those in steerage from those on

the upper decks was not to be bridged. First-class passengers might sometimes amuse themselves by touring below decks; but traffic in the other direction was unthinkable.

Compared to the experience of the earlier generations of emigrants, however, those who made the crossing around the turn of the century enjoyed accommodations that were almost civilized, due to the competition and stricter government controls. At the height of one rate war, for instance, North German Lloyd even offered to lend every steerage passenger an enameled dinner service, a spoon, and a fork, and proffered a blanket that could be taken away at the end of the voyage. By the early 1900s, government regulations stated that each passenger was to be supplied with a separate berth and "with as much provisions as he can eat, which are all of the best quality, and which are . . . cooked and served out by the company's servants." Medical care aboard the bigger liners got to be so good that emigrant women often tried to plan their crossing for the last days of pregnancy, so their babies could be delivered in the ship's infirmary. In their eagerness to reach America, the emigrants would have taken any accommodations they could get; but what they got was considerably better than steerage fifty years earlier.

A shipload of Eastern Europeans, part of the new wave of emigrants who traveled to America at the turn of the century, pour out of steerage to catch their first glimpse of the Promised Land.

As rivalry increased and government regulations became more stringent, steamship companies were forced to become more involved in passenger welfare; in the photo opposite, officers of the French Line inspect potential emigrants for trachoma, an infectious eye disease. Companies also set up agencies in neighboring countries which arranged, in addition to ship passage, feeder transportation to the debarkation port. A typical journey is outlined in the steerage contract (below, left), written in Swedish for the Liverpool-based Guion Line. Hamburg–America went even further when it set up a model village (below) to accommodate waiting emigrants, providing them with fumigation, a laundry, a brass band, and police protection.

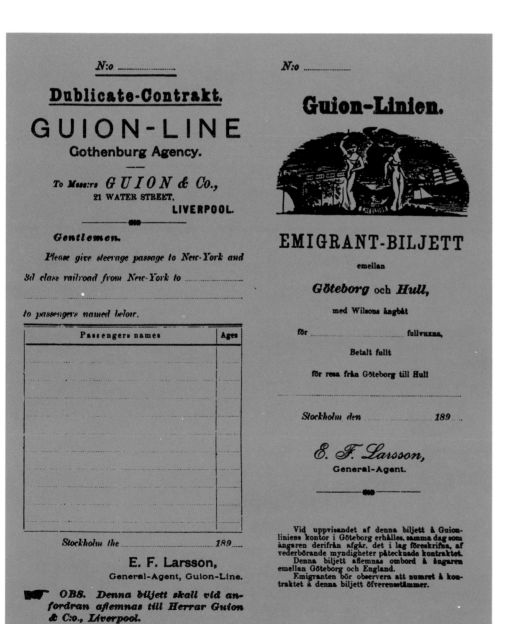

Emigration fever touched all segments of
European society and apparently all ages.
Trying to reach America without a ticket,
the small shoeless boy above, having been
caught as a stowaway, awaits the verdict
of three ship's officers. Would-be brides,
who set off for America in large numbers,
included those who are shown in the
photograph above (right)—a few of
the one thousand or more young women
who sailed together in September, 1907,
aboard White Star's *Baltic*. Emigrants
crowding the deck (opposite) were
photographed aboard the Red Star Line's
Westernland, circa 1890. As no deck space
was formally set aside, steerage passengers
had to find what comfort they could amid
the hawsers and hatch covers.

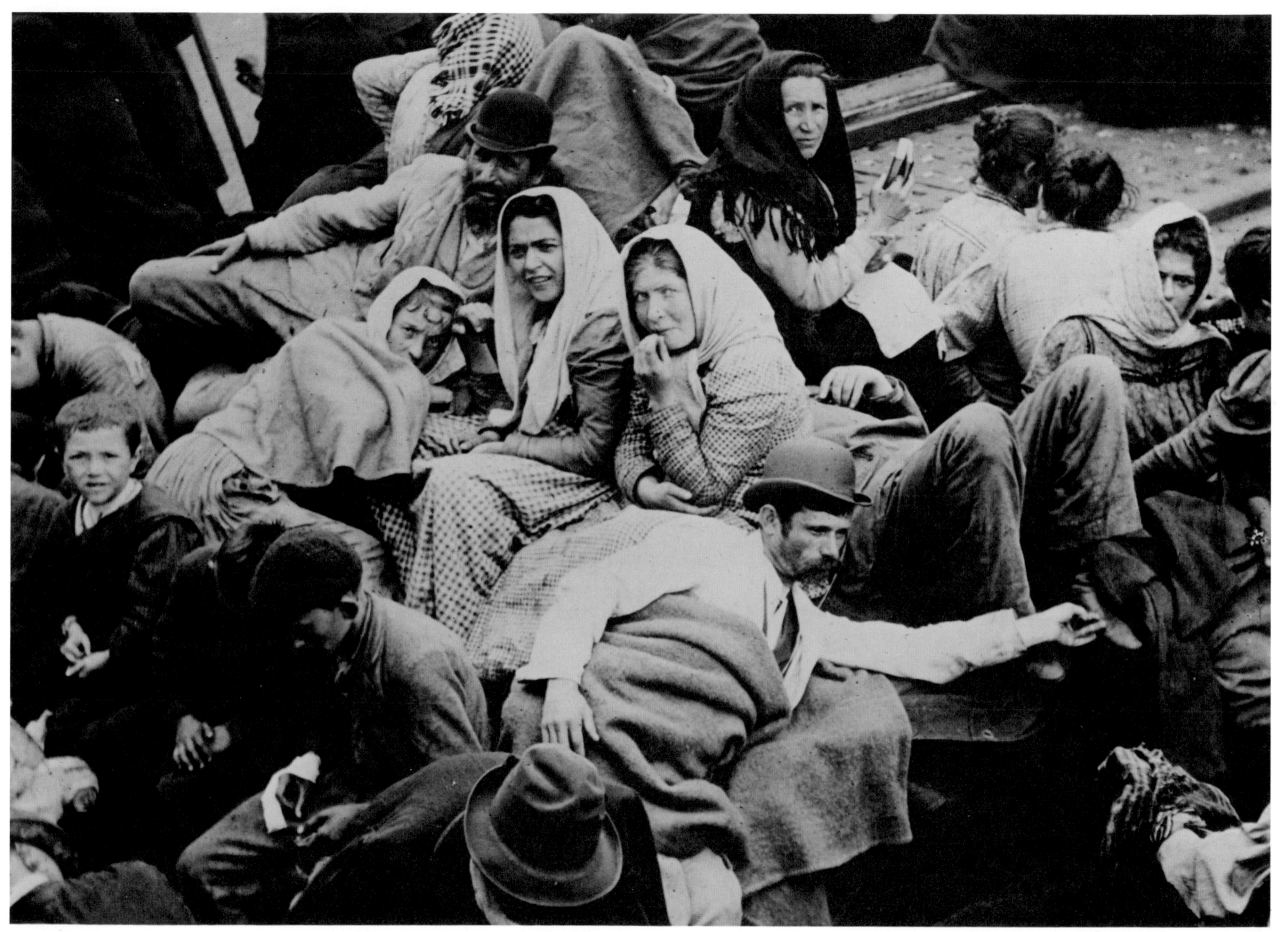

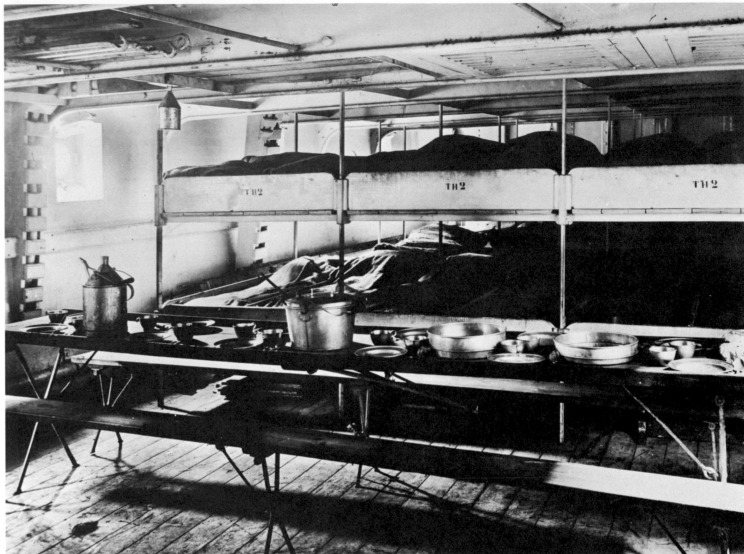

The 422 first-class passengers on the 1906 maiden voyage of the French Line's *La Provence* found such luxurious accommodations as a gilded dining saloon (left). Should they venture to go slumming on the decks below (a breech of company regulations and of good taste), they would find that steerage was another world altogether. Eight hundred third-class passengers lived in several sleeping-eating quarters like the one above. Unlike earlier emigrant ships, however, *La Provence* and her contemporaries did have porthole ventilation and electric lights to lessen the claustrophobic effects of crowding. Steerage passengers were also provided with such small comforts as company-issued straw mattresses and eating utensils.

When Hamburg–America's *Vaterland*—
950 feet of ocean-going speed and comfort—came down the ways in 1913, third-
class passengers were treated to facilities
that came close to making the trip a
pleasure. In the well-equipped laundry
room (top left), emigrant women often
did the laundry for first-class passengers,
who were without their own laundry
facilities. A professional-looking kitchen
(center, left) was connected with the serving pantry (above), and uniformed
servants brought meals to a room reserved
for steerage dining. Indeed, the old
sleeping-dining barracks had been sup-
planted altogether, and the standard
steerage cabins (left) were relatively
uncrowded and were segregated by sex.

As their ship steamed slowly into New
York Harbor, emigrants-turned-immigrants
crowded the rails to get their first view
of the Statue of Liberty. Around the turn
of the century, scenes like the one shown
on the opposite page were repeated
hundreds of times. Once inside the harbor,
the ship docked at a Manhattan pier to
unload first- and second-class passengers
and to transfer immigrants to lighters
(right) that would carry them to Ellis
Island (above). Built on twenty-seven
acres of landfill in Upper New York Bay,
this flamboyant pile of red brick and
limestone took the place of Castle Garden
as America's chief immigration reception
station in 1892. It maintained its preeminence until it was phased out in 1954.

New arrivals at Ellis Island were herded in lots of about thirty into the examination hall (above), a maze of pipe-fenced pens, to await medical inspections and interrogation about their political views, destinations, and job prospects. Men and women were separated during the physical examinations, administered assembly-line fashion (far left). As one Ellis Island employee remembered: "Whenever a case aroused suspicion, the alien was set aside in a cage apart from the rest, for all the world like a segregated animal, and his coat lapel or shirt marked with colored chalk, the color indicating why he had been isolated." In the photograph at left, three generations of a Dutch family await their final release.

A microcosm of the world's people, Ellis Island was the funnel through which as many as five thousand people were passed in a day—more than twenty million in the sixty-two years of its existence. The new Americans who are shown on this page were photographed during their passage through this historic gateway. In counter-clockwise order beginning left they include: a rabbi pausing in his reading; a Hungarian mother and her brood wearing the costume of their village; a group of North African women; a babushkaed Czech woman and her children; a group of Italians; and a Syrian woman bedecked with amber beads. Immigrants who failed inspection faced a long voyage home on the next ship.

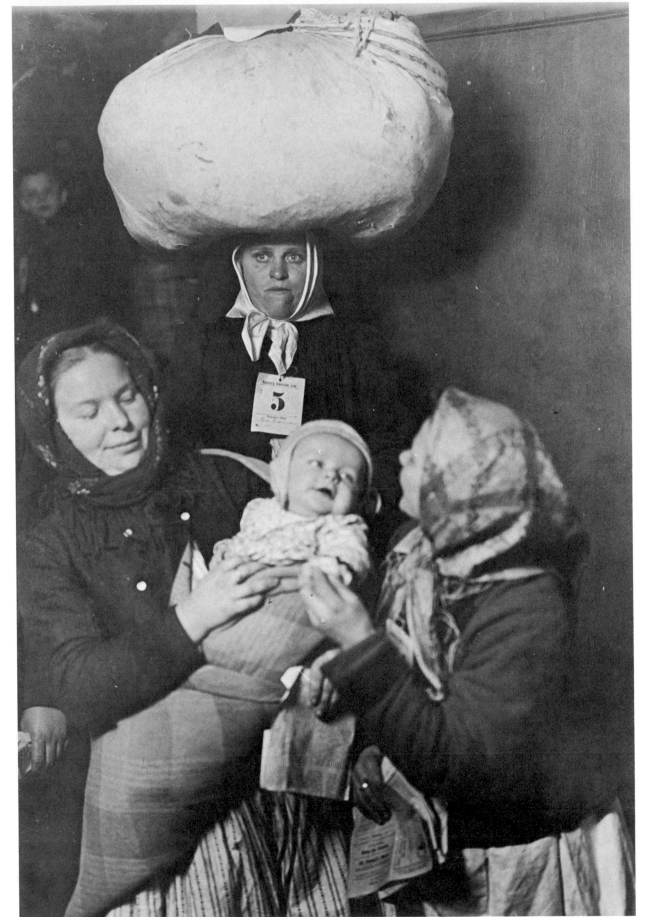

Balancing all her belongings atop her head, the Slavic woman (right) muses, perhaps, about the strange new life that lies across the harbor. The ticket tied to her coat informs the immigration officers that she has arrived on one of the Hamburg–America Line's ships and is listed on Manifest 5, Line 10 of their passenger registry. Many immigrants lost their old names permanently, being given "easier" American names by immigration officials. The Italian family (far right) has passed inspection and been transported by the Ellis Island ferry to a Manhattan pier. With railroad tickets clenched in their teeth and a look of triumph on their faces, they are experiencing their first moments on American soil.

Floating Palaces

1890–1909

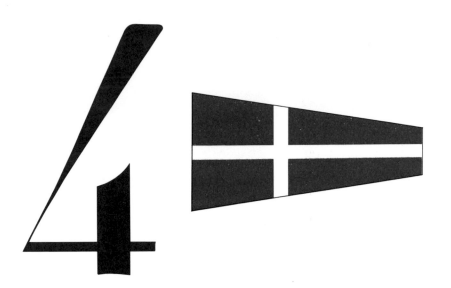

Steamships put to sea in high Victorian style . . . and new technology changes the look of the liner, which ceases to resemble the sailing ship that gave it birth. . . . Sails disappear, steel hulls replace wood and iron, and new decks are added, one on top of another. . . . Luxury becomes the keynote in the competition for passenger revenue, and well-to-do travelers bask in palatial splendor. . . . Cunard and White Star set the pace in speed and opulence . . . until Germany launches the *Kaiser Wilhelm der Grosse*, inaugurating a whole new class of express luxury liners. . . . Then, for a decade, the sleek German "greyhounds" reign supreme.

Saluting one another's good taste, passengers dally in the grand saloon of an Inman liner. In the late eighties, Inman's *City of Paris* and *City of New York* were the *sine qua non* of elegance and speed.

The Emperor was impressed. His Imperial Majesty, Wilhelm II of Germany, an honored guest at Britain's 1889 Naval Review, had just spent an hour and a half being conducted through the White Star Line's newest steamship, the *Teutonic*. He had seen the ship's voluptuous Victorian interior, with its leather-covered walls, its mahogany woodwork, its mirrors and murals, its plush settees. He had been apprised of the power of the ship's engines and generators, which provided electricity for the ship's lights and signals as well as for the electric hairbrushes in the ship's barber shop.

But most striking of all was the *Teutonic*'s uncluttered profile: she was one of the first steamships to abandon sails and rely on steam power alone. Clearly, the ship was a triumph. That the Emperor thought so became apparent when, at the end of his tour, he was overheard to say: "We must have some of these."

By 1889, the Atlantic liner had come a long way from the days when steam had provided only auxiliary power to wind and sail. Gradually, sail had become auxiliary to steam, being used mainly as a reserve source of power in case of an engine failure. But the chance of a complete engine breakdown was greatly reduced by the development of twin screws, double drive shafts, and double engines—innovations first used in the steamship trade in the late 1880s aboard Inman's prestigious *City of Paris* and *City of New York*. After that it was only a matter of time before sails disappeared altogether from the North Atlantic liners.

In this new era, the steamship bore little resemblance to the sailing ship that had given it birth. Steel hulls replaced wood and iron. Elegant clipper bows gave way to straight stems. The development of steam-powered steering gear, used successfully for the first time on the *Great Eastern* in 1866, meant that the wheelhouse could be moved forward thereby giving the helmsman better visibility.

Then, too, with the elimination of working masts and sails, it became possible to begin roofing over the decks and to build up the ship's superstructure. In the fierce competition for size and elegance that developed at the turn of the century, decks were piled one on top of another, until liners like the *Mauretania* and the *Titanic* were towering seven and eight decks high.

All this demanded huge investments of capital—much more than any one family or small partnership could manage. Shipping had become big business. As a result, there was a general trend toward reorganizing the old firms into limited liability companies, beginning as early as 1875, when the Inman Line went public. Five years later, the Cunard line was reorganized. (The company had remained in the control of Sir Samuel's family after his death in 1865.) The Guion Line followed suit in 1886, soon after its founder's death.

The building of larger and more efficient ships also meant that ever increasing numbers of passengers were needed to keep the big ships afloat. The best customers of the steamship lines were undoubtedly the emigrants who, in 1890, paid an average of only £4 (about $20), but who sometimes outnumbered first-class passengers by five to one. Yet the rivalry for passengers among the steamship lines made luxury and ornament an increasingly important part of the battle for passengers; and it was toward the comfort and convenience of first-class passengers (whose fares averaged £22 or $110) that the shipbuilders of the era strained their imaginations and directed their energies.

Long past were the days when Cunard could attract well-paying customers by offering "a plain cabin—nothing for show." Now there were electric bells for summoning the steward, and electric lights were to be found not only in the saloon but even

In the photo opposite, Kaiser Wilhelm follows Thomas Ismay (right) on an 1889 tour of the White Star Line's *Teutonic.* The Kaiser's covetous admiration was no doubt pleasing to her builders, Harland & Wolff of Belfast, whose board of directors, shown here, included G. W. Wolff (left) and Sir Edward Harland (right). Because the *Teutonic* and her successors had no need for sails, deck space was now freed from the crowding of masts and rigging (bottom left) and broad expanses were opened for sitting, strolling, and game playing, as shown in the scene (bottom right) made aboard the *Kaiser Wilhelm II.* The deck became, in the words of a contemporary, "a promenade likened by a New Yorker to a public park."

in private staterooms.

Cunard's *Lucania,* built in 1893 to rival White Star's *Teutonic,* set a new standard for opulence on the North Atlantic. With accommodations for 450 first-class (and 1000 steerage) passengers, the *Lucania* was equipped with elevators, palm courts, coal-burning fireplaces in all the principal rooms, and cabins *en suite*—that is, cabins in pairs with a sitting room between them. According to one contemporary description, the *Lucania's* public rooms suggested "the stately chambers of a palace rather than accommodation within the steel walls of a ship."

Nor were the British the only luxury shipwrights of the era. The Inman, French, and Holland–America lines were all taking steps to improve their saloon accommodations. But at the end of the century, the whole field was outclassed when Germany launched a new fleet of express liners that were faster and more luxurious than anything yet seen on the Western Ocean. The "greyhounds," as these long, narrow, and speedy ships were aptly called, ushered in an age of German supremacy on the North Atlantic. Much to the regret of English shipping men it was a supremacy that had been spurred at least in part by the Kaiser's tour of the *Teutonic* that summer afternoon in 1889.

An 1886 *Harper's Magazine* article stressed that liner captains were "emphatically Duty's children, even if obedience be at the expense . . . of life itself." But since the "captain almost invariably influences the passengers' choice of ship," public relations became a duty second only to safe sailing. Accordingly, the article went on to detail the physical and social peculiarities of several masters, including the three at right. Cunard's gruff Captain Judkins was to be avoided; White Star's Perry had snob appeal, having come "perhaps from the same family of Neptunes" as Commodore Perry; and Cunard's popular McMickan had a taste for hard liquor, talent as a storyteller, and "an eye of admiration for the gentle sex."

C. H. E. Judkins

H. Perry

W. McMickan

Well-heeled passengers capable of admiring the simple grace of the *Teutonic*'s long, sleek silhouette (opposite, above) were equally capable of appreciating the heavy, Byzantine opulence of her interior and giving themselves over to the lavish blandishments of her staff. The *Campania,* launched in 1892, carried 61 sailors, 22 engineers, 114 stewards, 45 cooks, and a 173-member black-gang, as the stokehole crew was called. The most visible staffers, of course, were the captain and his officers like the *Teutonic*'s complement posed on the bridge (above, left) and the able-bodied seamen (left). Rarely seen but indispensable were the cooks (above) and the crewmen who toiled in the stokehole, shoveling the liners across the Atlantic.

The bedchamber at top (right) was typical of the accommodations offered to first-class passengers aboard White Star's *Teutonic*. It was this kind of luxury that the Cunard Line sought to surpass when it ordered the superships *Campania* and *Lucania,* which took the Blue Ribbon from White Star in 1893. As noted by one traveler, "the domestic architect was called into service, entrusted to dispel the idea that one was really on board ship, in favor of the illusion that one was really living in a luxurious hotel."

The designers' success is evident in the photograph on the opposite page, which shows the *Lucania*'s magnificent dining saloon. A graphic illustration of what money could buy at the turn of the century, the room was described by a Cunard enthusiast as "highly artistic, neither gaudy nor oppressively elaborate."

As the last word in luxe and speed, and aided by posters like the one at left, the *Campania* and *Lucania* gained a popularity that outlived their supremacy. By way of contrast to the first-class accommodations of the period, second-class passengers aboard Cunard's *Saxonia* occupied cabins like the one at right (middle); while a smoking room was now provided for steerage passengers aboard the better liners (right, bottom). A few years earlier Robert Louis Stevenson had found the chief difference between steerage and second class to be that "in steerage there are males and females; in the second cabin, ladies and gentlemen."

Passengers aboard the liners of the 1890s seemed content with simple amusements. Energetic types played "shovelboard" (as the game was then being called). Others could spend hours staring dreamily out to sea, as the young lady seems to be doing in the watercolor at right. But the most popular sport was promenading. The couple opposite are clearly having a high time; while the Victorians below have paused in the midst of the day's activities to have their picture taken. But there were pitfalls aboard, too. One young woman wrote that "one of the awful Cook's tourists men came up and asked me 'if I hadn't thrown up yet.'" *Harper's* told of a captain who, "whenever the ship's concert is held, endears himself to the passengers by singing 'I'm afloat, I'm afloat, and the Rover is Free.'" Another observer warned of the dangers of the smoking room aboard the *Campania:* "At one end is its special bar, and tables for . . . a quiet game of dominoes, backgammon, or whist, where, alas, 'contrary to rules,' the professional gambler may quietly empty the purse of some green fellow traveler."

The German "Greyhounds" Take the Lead

In September, 1897, Germany put an abrupt end to Britain's long domination of the North Atlantic luxury service. The Germans were already the leaders in the emigrant trade, with North German Lloyd alone carrying three-quarters of a million emigrants to America in the 1880s—twice as many as either Cunard or White Star. Now, in the year when Britons all over the Empire were celebrating the sixtieth anniversary of Queen Victoria's reign and the glory of British supremacy over land and sea, along came a ship which, at one stroke, rendered all of Britain's prestigious luxury liners obsolete.

The new liner was the *Kaiser Wilhelm der Grosse* (pictured at right). The first non-British ship since the Collins paddlers of the 1850s to hold the Blue Ribbon record for the fastest Atlantic crossing, she made an average trip in five and a half days. A gleaming black and white giant, with four funnels arranged in pairs, she was adorned inside like a floating Rhine castle, with stained glass windows, cathedral ceilings, and a plethora of paintings, carvings, and bas-reliefs.

The success of the *Wilhelm* cast an aura of glamour over the whole North German Lloyd fleet, and secured for the company the cream of all transatlantic passenger traffic. Kaiser Wilhelm II can hardly be

blamed for gloating. "This," he said, "is a salutary lesson to every rival maritime nation."

During the next decade, German preeminence on the North Atlantic was unquestioned, as one prestige liner after another slid down the ways of the German shipyards at Stettin and Danzig: the *Deutschland,* which entered service in 1900; the *Kronprinz Wilhelm* (1901); the *Kaiser Wilhelm II* (1903); the Belfast-built *Amerika* (1905), which is shown in the poster at left; and the *Kronprinzessen Cecilie* (1907).

Fast and luxurious, the German greyhounds were powered by huge multistage engines forty feet high, which represented the ultimate advance in the reciprocating engine first developed by James Watt in the 1770s. They were among the first ships to use three engines and three screws. And they were also among the first to be equipped with ship-to-shore wireless sets—short-range affairs used mostly for announcing arrivals.

Germany's pack of greyhounds thoroughly outclassed every other ship on the Atlantic, leaving the top liners of Britain, France, and Holland in their wakes. For a time, at least, rivalry for the speed record was strictly a German affair, fought out between Hamburg–America and North German Lloyd.

The builders of the *Kaiser Wilhelm der Grosse,* who guaranteed to take her back if she did not win the Blue Ribbon, not only won their gamble but produced a new set of steamship firsts in a decade that had already seen an incredible number of them. Her extraordinarily long, four-funneled profile set the pattern for a new generation of liners. Her saloon, smoking room (left), staterooms, and bathrooms were higher, bigger, and more ornate than any ever before set afloat; she held more passengers and had bigger engines. Despite a knowledgeable British opinion that a wireless was an "absurd suggestion," the inventor, Guglielmo Marconi, was hired, and the *Wilhelm der Grosse* became the first big European liner with a radio.

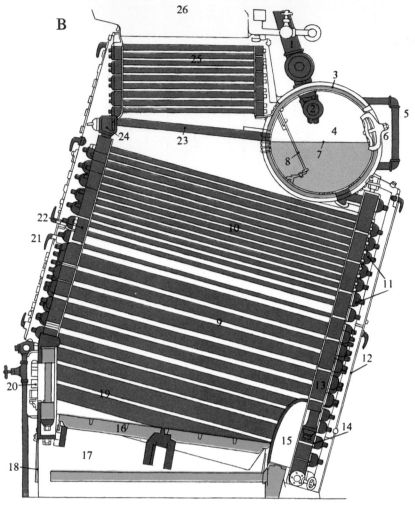

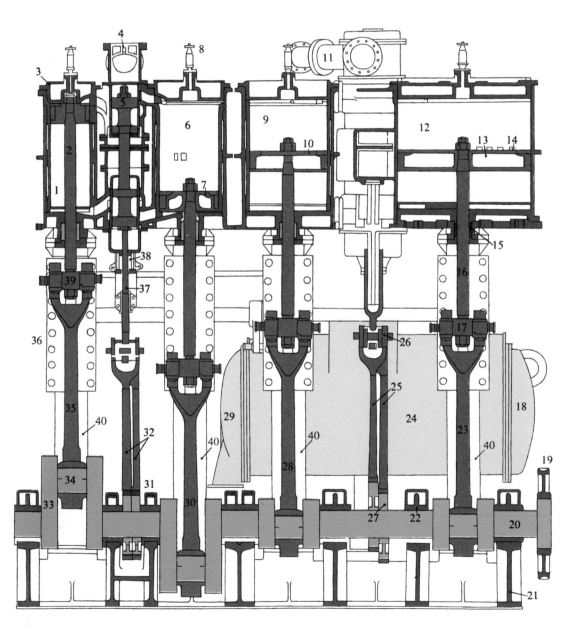

Schematic drawings of a quadruple-expansion engine (left) and a boiler (above) are shown here.

Water flowing into the tube banks of the boiler (9, 10) is heated and collected as steam in the steam space (4), the water having undergone a sixteen-hundredfold expansion during its conversion to steam. The steam is released to a compressor, where it is dried by a superheater and then is admitted under high pressure (213 pounds per square inch) into the smallest cylinder of the engine (1, at left). The steam exhausted from the first cylinder then goes on to cylinders of increasingly greater diameter (6, 9, 12), a greater surface area being needed for each suc-cessive stage in order to utilize the ever decreasing pressure of the steam. Crankshafts are used to transfer the power from the pistons' up-and-down thrusts to rotary motion for the propeller shaft.

The man in the foreground in the engraving (opposite) of the *Kaiser Wilhelm der Grosse*'s engine indicates the monstrous size of the machines. The German quadruple-expansion engines stood forty feet high. To keep the engines moving, eighty men at a time hand-fed thirty tons of coal an hour to 120 boilers. The giant engines were the ultimate reciprocating engines, and almost before they had been installed they were as doomed as the dinosaurs.

NORDD. LLOYD, BREMEN

Schnelldampfer „Kronprinz Wilhelm"

Kapitän A. Richter

Please give Uncle George my love. There is lots of vibration on this boat—

Captains of the German liners pushed their mighty engines to the furthest limits that the machinery and weather would allow with results that both pleased and discomfited their passengers. The postcard at left highlights the problem. But promoters of the lines were always careful to present their ships—and the stormy North Atlantic —in the best possible light. Artists for North German Lloyd and Hamburg–America have done just that in the turn-of-the-century graphics shown on these pages. Only ships on tranquil seas were shown in promotion folders such as those on the opposite page.

Meanwhile, a sense of gracious elegance pervades the modish Art Nouveau menu covers at right and at left, below. The latter, the cover of a menu from the *Kronprinz Wilhelm,* is as pure Art Nouveau as the inside is Art Ancien. Diners who partook of that dinner had purchased a ticket "with meals." A popular innovation aboard Hamburg–America's new liners was a "no-meal" ticket, which allowed passengers to eat in the shipboard Ritz-Carlton restaurant at any hour they pleased. In that elegant ambience they could enjoy the most particular personal service and a special à la carte menu.

Hamburg-Amerika Linie

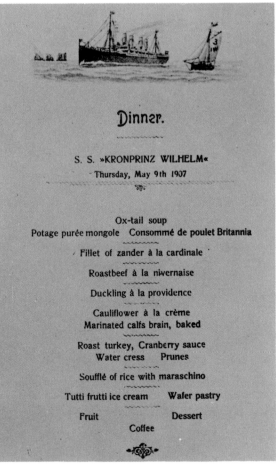

Norddeutscher Lloyd Bremen.

Dinner.

S. S. »KRONPRINZ WILHELM«
· Thursday, May 9th 1907 ·

Ox-tail soup
Potage purée mongole   Consommé de poulet Britannia

· Fillet of zander à la cardinale ·

Roastbeef à la nivernaise

Duckling à la providence

Cauliflower à la crème
Marinated calfs brain, baked

Roast turkey, Cranberry sauce
Water cress   Prunes

Soufflé of rice with maraschino

Tutti frutti ice cream   Wafer pastry

Fruit   Dessert

Coffee

Norddeutscher Lloyd
Bremen.

1905

Norddeutscher Lloyd
Bremen

Edition française.

OCTOBER, 1907

NORTH
GERMAN
LLOYD
BULLETIN

The chief competitor of North German
Lloyd at the turn of the century was the
Hamburg–America Line. Operating out of
the port of Hamburg, (above, center), it
was the world's largest shipping company,
with 431 vessels afloat in 1914. Its success
could be directly attributed to the brilliant
Albert Ballin (left), a *wünderkind* who,
by the time he was thirty-one, had risen
from a job in a small Hamburg shipping
agency to become the director of the Hamburg–America Line itself. Ballin was one of
the cleverest wheeler-dealers of his day.
Sensing trends before they started, he had
the foresight to designate some steerage
space "tourist class" when the flood of sightseers was just beginning. And through his
powerful connections in the government
he was able to insure that emigrants
from Eastern Europe could not clear
German health inspections unless they
were traveling on ships of the Hamburg–
America line.

The star of the Hamburg–America Line at the turn of the century was the long, low, four-funneled *Deutschland*. Shown charging through the Atlantic in the poster on the opposite page, the ship captured the Blue Ribbon in 1900 and with it the attention of the public. The *Deutschland*, however, was pushed so hard that there were constant boiler and vibration problems, and in 1910 she was demoted to cruising status. The decision was no doubt applauded by the ship's passengers, two of whom are posed dourly on deck in the photo above. Thereafter, Ballin followed Britain's lead in emphasizing comfort rather than speed. One result of the new policy was the luxurious *Amerika* shown in the cross section at left. The splendid Ritz-Carlton Restaurant, its roof rising two decks high, is seen just beneath the bridge at top center. Five decks below is the warren of three-tiered bunk beds that accommodated 2300 steerage passengers.

Charles Mewès, looking every inch the artiste in the photograph at upper left, was another of Ballin's coups. Impressed by the quiet opulence of the new Ritz-Carlton Grill in London, Ballin sought out Mewès, its decorator, who was delighted to accept the challenge of shipboard design. Mewès' plans for the *Amerika* marked the first time a ship's interiors achieved a uniformity of design due to its execution by a single architect. After that, Mewès had so many commissions that he never found time to make the Atlantic crossing and bask in his own elegance before his death in 1914. His dramatic, double-curved stairway (above) and the public room (left) adorned Hamburg–America's pacesetter, the *Kaiserin Auguste Victoria*.

The vulgar flamboyance of the decor of
ships built in the 1880s and 1890s was
stifling to some; to be sure, the majority
thought it the *ne plus ultra* in elegance
and taste. As Mark Twain noted during a
turn-of-the century crossing: "Everywhere
I find sumptuous masses of color . . . and
as a result the ship is bright and cheery to
the eye, and this cheeriness invades one's
spirit and contents it." Mewès, in his interiors, employed a more subtle extravagance. He loved the pure lines and subtle
colors of the late eighteenth century,
particularly the period of Louis XVI, and
this style often appeared in Hamburg–
America liners. In contrast, after the turn
of the century, North German Lloyd opened
the portholes and let in some fresh air. Art
Nouveau's time had come. Shown here are
a staircase and a first-class dining room on
the line's S.S. *George Washington,* where
the emphasis was on linear grace and
straightforward simplicity.

Into the Modern Age

1897–1914

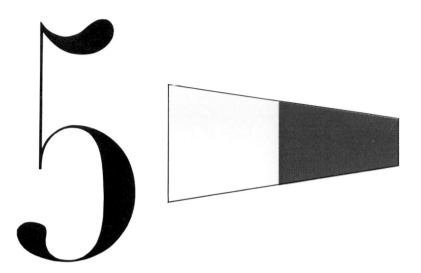

The turbine engine, powerhouse of the future, makes a dramatic debut aboard a vessel named *Turbinia* . . . and scandalizes the British Admiralty. . . . J. P. Morgan makes his bid to take over the entire North Atlantic . . . and Cunard, fighting for its life, launches the *Mauretania* and *Lusitania*, splendid liners that promptly shatter every size and speed record. . . . On the new turbine liners, where the accent is on elegance for those who can afford it, new money rubs shoulders with old . . . and the "unsinkable" *Titanic*, promising a new era of safety and speed, meets disaster. . . . Yet the battle for supremacy at sea rages as fiercely as ever.

Streaking through the British fleet during the celebration of Queen Victoria's Diamond Jubilee in June, 1897, the *Turbinia* gives the world its first astonished look at what turbine engines can do. Moving faster than any vessel had yet traveled at sea—34½ knots, almost 40 land miles an hour—she dashed in and out of the fleet at will. "Her speed," reported *The Times,* "was simply astonishing, but its manifestation was accompanied by a mighty rushing sound and by a stream of flame from her funnel at least as long as the funnel itself." The *Turbinia* was so fast that when outraged naval officers sent a picket boat to intercept her, the picket nearly foundered in her wake. *Turbinia*'s power was a set of three turbines, one of which—barely ten feet long—is shown at right. Three propellers were attached to each turbine's drive shift. Their design was tested as thoroughly as the turbines themselves.

For transatlantic express liners the modern era began with a bang in June, 1897. It was then that British engineer Charles Algernon Parsons gave the maritime world its first glimpse of a new method of marine propulsion that was to revolutionize ocean travel: the steam turbine.

Having developed and tested his invention in secret, Parsons carefully chose the moment for the unveiling. "If you believe in a principle," he later wrote, "never damage it with a poor expression. You must go the whole way. I had to startle people."

Parsons' golden opportunity came during the 1897 Naval Review which, like everything else that year in Britain, was being held in honor of Queen Victoria's Diamond Jubilee. With pennants flying, the home fleet had lined up for inspection by the Prince of Wales and the lords of the Admiralty. The Kaiser's nephew, Prince Henry of Prussia, was also present. And on shore, the Queen herself was watching through a telescope. The royal yacht was just beginning her stately progress through the fleet when Parsons' *Turbinia* came shooting from the sidelines across her wake.

The Admiralty was appalled by the intrusion, but the demonstration was a spectacular success. Thanks to Parsons, Britain now possessed the means to

regain her supremacy from Germany. As the *Daily Mail* predicted in its report of the *Turbinia*'s escapade: "If that shrimp of a turbinet comes to anything, all these black and yellow leviathans are done for."

The turbine engine displayed so dramatically by Parsons that afternoon was the culmination of years of research. Beginning with experiments in turbine-driven electrical power generators, Parsons had developed his first turbine in 1884. Utilizing a principle known for centuries, he had sought to harness the reaction power of steam exhaust by focusing jets of steam upon a series of bladed disks that were attached to a crankshaft. The power of the steam caused the disks—and hence the shaft—to rotate at a high velocity.

There were a number of difficulties that had to be overcome before this principle could be applied to ship propulsion. Chief among them was the problem of moderating the speed of the spinning turbine to an efficient level; otherwise the propeller attached to the shaft spun too fast to develop adequate thrust in the water. But by 1895, Parsons was conducting the *Turbinia*'s first secret trials in the North Sea, and two years later he sprang his invention upon the startled world.

Within a short time, the Admiralty, swallowing its

pride, ordered two experimental destroyers equipped with turbines: H.M.S. *Cobra* and H.M.S. *Viper*. In 1904, the *Victorian*, built for Canada's Allan Line, became the first turbine-powered passenger liner on the North Atlantic. A year later, Cunard's *Carmania* and *Caronia* made their maiden voyages, one powered by turbines and the other by conventional engines. The *Carmania*'s turbines, smaller and lighter than the mammoth reciprocating engines then being used in big liners, proved so superior in speed and fuel economy that Cunard went ahead with plans to install turbines in their two new Blue Ribbon challengers, the soon-to-be-famous sisters, *Mauretania* and *Lusitania*.

The two ships were built to be winners, and Britain's maritime reputation was badly in need of winners. In 1900, when Hamburg–America was the biggest line in the world and had ninety-five steamers at sea, Cunard had only eight ships on the North Atlantic, fewer than at any time since the early 1850s. The supremacy of the German liners was so overwhelming that when in 1899 White Star introduced its prestige luxury liner *Oceanic*—the first ship to exceed the length of the *Great Eastern*—no attempt was made to compete for the speed record. Instead, White Star emphasized the ship's size and comfort

J. P. Morgan, caught in a ferocious moment
in the photo opposite, left, inadvertently
spurred the rejuvenation of Britain's
merchant marine. When White Star fell
into Morgan's pocket and even Cunard
seemed likely to be "[M]organized,"
Cunard's directors used the take-over
attempt to win the government subsidies
they needed to build a prize-winning
fleet. Claiming to be helpless before the
manipulations of this rapacious American,
they stirred the chauvinist in every
Englishman. Cartoons like the one opposite,
right, were common in the press, and street
vendors, appealing to the wry English wit,
did a lively business selling licenses to
remain on earth—supposedly signed by
the all-powerful J. Pierpont Morgan.

and praised the pleasures of a leisurely crossing.

Then, in 1902, came a new blow to British prestige,
when American financier J. P. Morgan acquired the
great White Star Line, incorporating it into his
fast-growing International Mercantile Marine company. Attempting to gain the kind of monopoly
over Atlantic shipping that he already held over
America's railroads, Morgan had been buying up one
shipping line after another. Dominion, National,
Albion, Red Star, and Inman came under his banner,
as did a large share of Holland–America. The
Kaiser, always seeking an advantage over Britain,
had even allowed the great Hamburg–America Line to
join Morgan's combine as a most-favored competitor.

For a time it seemed that even Cunard would be
drawn into Morgan's net. But because the venerable
company, now ranked as a national institution, was
under threat of an American take-over, Parliament
voted the subsidy needed to keep Cunard British.
With these funds, Cunard was able to build its Blue
Ribbon contenders, introducing the *Mauretania* and
Lusitania in 1907. These two vessels were the largest
and the fastest yet built, and they immediately and
decisively returned Great Britain to preeminence on
the North Atlantic. Together they ushered in a new
era of steamship elegance.

The sleek *Turbinia*, 100 feet long but
only nine feet wide, is seen here dashing
through the North Sea on a test run. The
turbine's inventor, Charles Parsons
(above) hardly looked the part of the
flashy entrepreneur, but it was his
imaginative introduction of the turbine
engine that gave the Cunard Line the
weapon it needed to battle Morgan's
International Mercantile Marine. Once
again, Cunard proved to be a powerful
adversary. Eventually, Morgan was to sell
the White Star Line back to British holders,
and in the early thirties the International
Mercantile Marine was to vanish from
the Atlantic. In the end, according to the
Wall Street Journal, "the ocean was too big
for the old man."

Two Legends Are Born: the *Lusitania* and *Mauretania*

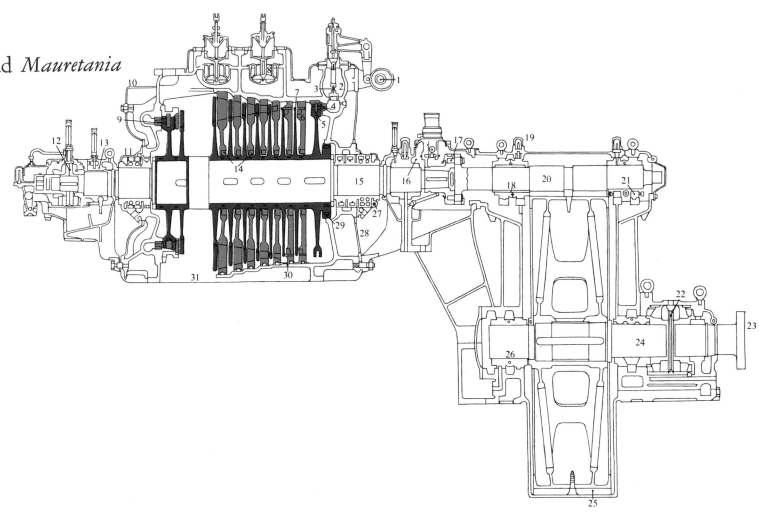

"Barring a bridle path for the equestrian, a smooth road for the automobilist, and a forest for lovers to walk in, everything seems to have been provided" aboard the *Mauretania,* wrote marine historian E. Keble Chatterton. Another writer, watching the *Lusitania* being built, thought it astonishing "that men could fashion such a thing by their hands out of metal and wood."

The English-built *Mauretania* and the Scottish-built *Lusitania* were indeed extraordinary ships. Named for ancient Roman provinces (Mauretania was in northwest Africa; Lusitania included modern Portugal), they entered service in 1907, only ten years after Charles Parsons' first public demonstration of the turbine engine.

Each ship rose eight decks high, was more than seven hundred fifty feet long, and carried more than two thousand passengers. Each was driven by four giant turbines, and generated fully seventy-five percent more power than the largest ship with reciprocating engines. Filling the bunkers in one of these giants required twenty-two trainloads of coal.

The *Mauretania* and the *Lusitania* were the first ships to cross the Atlantic in under five days. Of the two, the *Mauretania* was faster and luckier; her record was to remain unchallenged for twenty-two years.

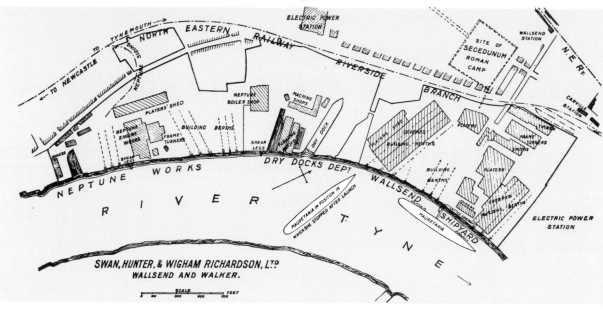

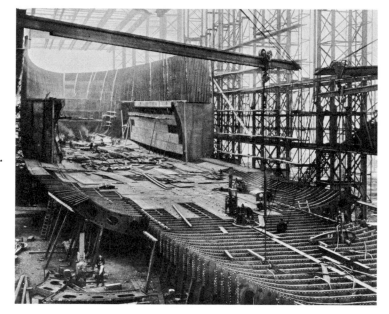

In contrast to the *Turbinia*'s ten-foot-long engine, one of the *Mauretania*'s low-pressure turbines was so big that it dwarfed an automobile (opposite, right). In another photo (opposite, left), the *Turbinia* appears to be a mere sliver beside her giant offspring.

As seen in the cutaway drawing of a modern turbine, rings of bladed disks mounted on a circular shaft rotate in a drum between similar but stationary disks. Steam, admitted from nozzles (4), causes rotation as it flows between the stationary and movable disks. As steam pressure decreases, the chamber widens out to absorb maximum energy. Since the direction in which the turbine turns cannot be reversed, a small reverse-turning engine

has to be added (9).

The panorama at top is of the Newcastle yards of Swan, Hunter, and Wigham Richardson, where the *Mauretania* was built. The seventy-eight-acre complex on the River Tyne is laid out in the map above, which shows the ship's launch path.

At center, the ship's hull takes shape inside the yard's iron-and-glass workshed. The ship's steel ribs, assembled in the yard, were hoisted into place by the cranes seen projecting from right and left. The double wall rising amidships is the protective inner skin of the coal bunkers. Farther forward can be seen the curve of the bow. About a year (and millions of rivets) after the ship's skeleton was laid, the massive plated hull was in place (far right).

A naval architect's 1907 plan (right) and cross section (left, above) show how the turbines and propeller shafts were seated in the *Mauretania*'s engine room; while the photo of her stern quarter (right, above), with the starboard screws in place, shows the grand realization of the architect's design.

As seen in the plan, high pressure turbines on the port and starboard turn the outboard screws. Steam that has passed through those turbines is diverted to the much larger, low pressure turbines that power the inboard screws. The direct coupling of the turbines and the propeller shafts was a drawback on the *Mauretania* and on other ships built before World War I. It meant that the turbines, which operate most efficiently at high speeds, had to turn at relatively low speeds in order to avoid a phenomenon called *cavitation*. This occurs when a rotative vacuum forms around a high speed propeller and water rushes in to fill it, causing terrible noise and vibration. Eventually Parsons solved the problem by adding a speed-reducing gear between the engine and shaft.

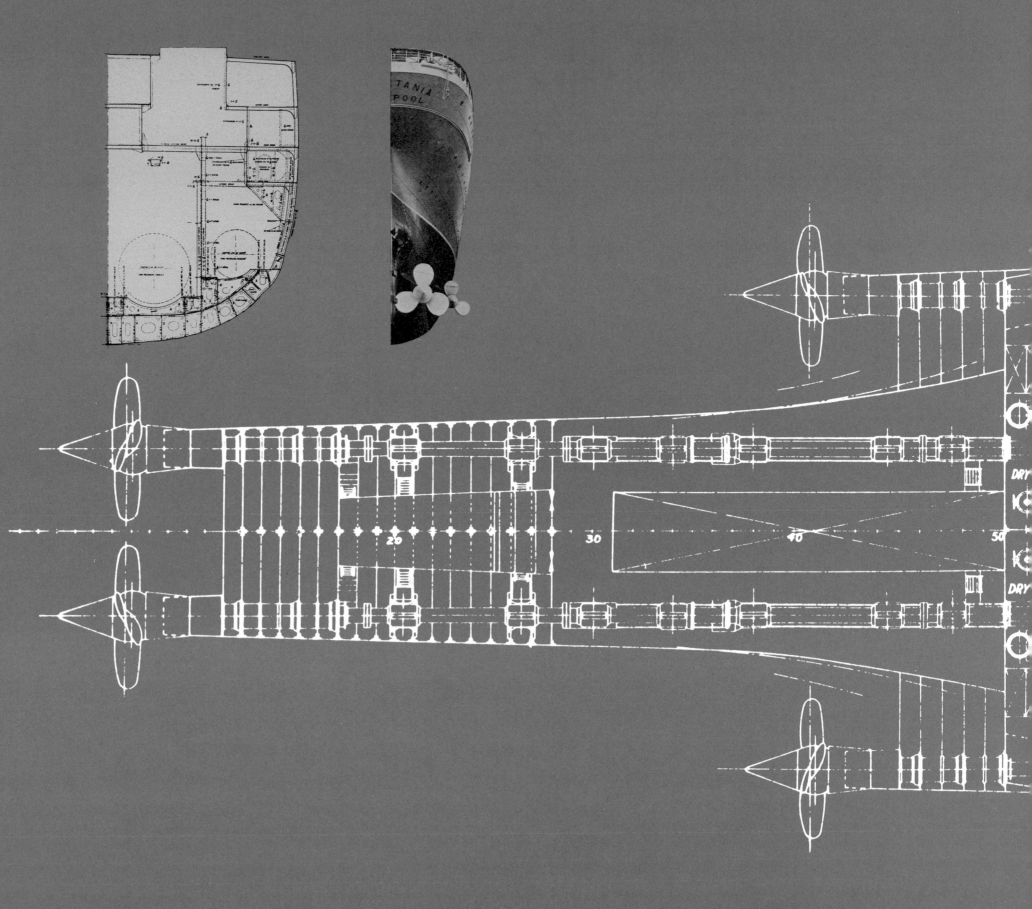

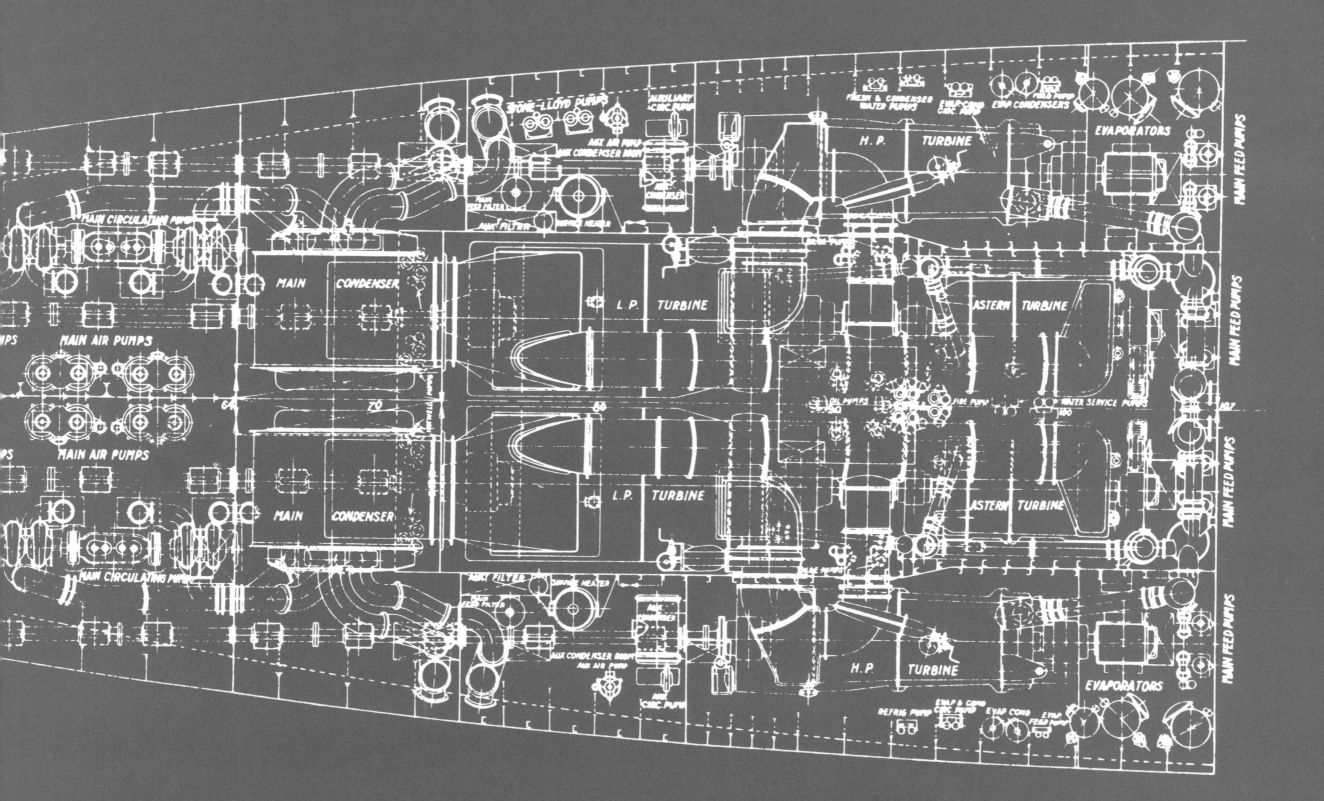

One of the most complicated aspects of completing giant ships like the *Mauretania* and *Lusitania* was the launch. The headlong rush down the skids had to be carefully controlled to prevent the monster from slamming into the opposite bank of the river. This sequence of photographs shows the launch of the *Lusitania* in June, 1906, at the Glasgow shipbuilding yards of John Brown, Ltd. The great wall of steel stood poised on the stocks (opposite page) until steel triggers and workmen swinging hammers had knocked away the last support timbers. The moment the ship's 16,000 tons hit the waters of the River Clyde, her speed was slowed by 80- to 100-ton coils of braided chains and weights, geared to give way little by little.

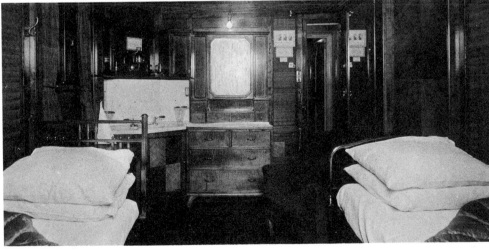

"The *Mauretania* has been described as the most costly decorated vessel afloat," wrote marine historian F. A. Talbot soon after the ship's launch. "But it is British in style, treatment, and workmanship, solid and durable, so that it fulfills national traditions." Critics found her muted compared to her predecessors; but as seen in photos of a two-room suite, the first-class dining room, and the paneling of the smoking room, the decor was lush and ornate.

The *Lusitania*'s first arrival in New York in September, 1907 (seen at left, off the Battery) caused a sensation, despite the fact that her captain had not run her full out. On her second trip, however, she brought the Blue Ribbon back to Britain, steaming from Queenstown (Cobh) to Sandy Hook in four days, nineteen hours, and fifty-two minutes, and taking only three hours more than that on her return. The *Mauretania* was seen off by a cheering crowd at Liverpool (above) on her maiden voyage, two months after her sister ship entered service. From the beginning, some indefinable quality made the *Mauretania* enormously popular, while her ill-fated sister remained the second choice of most travelers. "If there ever was a ship which possessed the thing called 'soul,' the *Mauretania* did," said Franklin Roosevelt. "As Captain Rostron once said to me, she had the manners and deportment of a great lady and behaved herself as such."

Life on Board in the New Century: Glamour, Games, and Lazy Afternoons

A symphony of sights, sounds, and smells cheered the departure of a liner: the smells of engine oil, the salty sea, and floorwax; the scraping of steamer trunks along the decks; the confusion of faces and voices; the slow, reluctant leaving of visitors to the cry of "All ashore that's going ashore"; and then the blast of the horn as the tugs eased the ship away from the dock. It was an experience shared by millions.

In the years before air travel, when ships were literally the only way to cross, transatlantic voyages were made by everybody who was anybody—and many more who weren't. Passenger lists included the famous names of politics and the arts, society and business, and the names of millions of anonymous individuals seeking new pleasures or new ways of life. Only the gigantic liners of the era made possible the huge numbers of emigrants that came pouring across the Atlantic in the first decades of the century, providing cheap and safe passage for upward of a thousand emigrants with each crossing.

Meanwhile, on the upper decks, first-class passengers were traveling with greater ease and comfort than ever before, and their numbers were swelled by troops of prosperous American sightseers, for whom a tour of Europe's resorts and cultural centers had become "the thing to do."

Of all the preparations for a voyage, the one the crew hated most was coaling. And they probably did not hate it nearly as much as the men who had to hand-load twenty-two trainsfull—seven thousand tons—of the fuel into a ship's bunkers. In the picture at left below, workmen at the Fourteenth Street Pier in New York hoist quarter-ton lots aboard the *Mauretania,* which burned a thousand tons of coal a day. The sooty fallout from the coaling-up penetrated everything no matter how carefully it was covered, forcing the crew to hose down the decks and clean and polish the ship before the passengers boarded. Then the stewards, like those on the Canadian Pacific's *Empress of Britain* (top left), could begin to sort the enormous quantities of trunks, valises, and satchels that customarily accompanied passengers on the Grand Tour.

Oblivious to the work that preceded their arrival, travelers and well-wishers climb the gangway (opposite, top), headed for bon voyage parties. Finally, the last visitor was shooed to the pier, there to wave friends and family out of sight—as in the photo opposite, right, which shows the crowd on the pierhead beside the *Olympic.* Then the longshoremen hauled in the gangways and cast off the mooring lines, and the tugs nudged the ship out into the stream. The tugs shown in the photograph opposite, left, belong to New York's most famous fleet of tugboats, the Moran fleet, which has shepherded the great ships into and out of their piers since 1860.

The Smart Set at Sea

In the first decades of the century, a steamship crossing was an economic necessity to some and a social imperative to others. The smart set of the time consisted of international businessmen and the moneyed aristocracy, who had connections on both sides of the Atlantic. Among the latter was Mrs. F. W. Vanderbilt, seen at left disembarking delicately in New York. Prominent actors, dancers, vaudevillians, and opera singers were also frequent passengers on the North Atlantic lines, and their presence on board lent an air of glamour to any voyage. (That's Enrico Caruso putting on the ritz, right.) On the best ships, the rich and famous were numerous enough to provide first-class celebrity-seekers with ample opportunity to bask in reflected glory. The ship's concert, inevitably chaired by a socially prominent gentleman, was especially popular when the succession of amateur performances was broken by a genuine star.

Soprano Luisa Tetrazzini

Andrew Carnegie

D. W. Griffith

Isadora Duncan

Nicholas and Alice Roosevelt Longworth

Vernon and Irene Castle

William Jennings Bryan and family

Caruso, Toscanini and Company

A few of the prominent passengers to be seen on the best liners in the early 1900s are shown on this page. Ohio congressman Nicholas Longworth and his bride Alice Roosevelt, daughter of the President, are seen above on their wedding trip to Europe in 1906. Mrs. Stanley McCormick (below) is on her way to a suffragist conference in London. At left, an all-star cast of opera greats poses during a 1914 voyage from Naples to Boston aboard White Star's *Canopic*. Among them are: Caruso (down front, in beret); over his left shoulder, conductor Arturo Toscanini; Amelita Galli–Curci (directly above Toscanini); Freda Hempel (over the maestro's left shoulder); and to her left, Emma Eames. Geraldine Farrar and Lina Cavalieri are the ladies at left.

Theodore Roosevelt

Sarah Bernhardt

Vaslav Nijinsky and family

John D. Rockefeller

Mrs. Stanley McCormick

The pace of life during a transatlantic crossing varied according to each passenger's mood and energy. The deck chair commodores aboard Canada's *Empress of Britain* (opposite) indulge in perhaps the most popular pastime, while aboard the rolling *Lusitania* (left) a pair of gentlemen take an angular promenade, seemingly oblivious to having disrupted a shuffle-board game. For more active types, there were helter-skelter three-legged races (top left) and games of deck tennis, as shown above. For such active passengers as these the liners began supplying sports equipment early in the century, but adults were still responsible for organizing their own fun; the *Imperator,* however, provided a social director for children (top).

"CQD SOS Come at Once. We Have Struck a Berg."

THE SINKING OF THE TITANIC

CAREFULLY DRAWN FROM SKETCHES AND DESCRIPTIONS OF EYE WITNESSES:— THE SCENE ABOUT 40 MINUTES BEFORE THE FINAL PLUNGE.

With the world waiting tensely for details of the *Titanic*'s disaster, the editors of the *New York Evening Sun,* lacking hard facts, chose to rely on the White Star Line's reassurances (opposite). The picture at left was one of the many graphic portrayals made when the full extent of the tragedy became known.

"Unsinkable," they called her with an unbounded faith in the achievements of engineering and man. The largest ship in the world, White Star's *Titanic* had a double bottom and sixteen watertight compartments. She could stay afloat with any two of the compartments flooded. But on the night of April 14, 1912, while speeding for New York on her maiden voyage with 2,207 souls on board, the ship took a raking underwater blow from an iceberg. Five of her forward compartments were ripped open below the waterline and the sea came roaring in. Three hours later she slid under, bow first. In keeping with out-dated regulations, she carried lifeboats for only half her passengers.

Outraged by the needless tragedy, Joseph Conrad, like many others, laid the blame on "what the steamship companies considered to be 'the travelling public's demand for size, luxury, and speed—speed above all things.'"

Hard lessons were learned from this, the worst sea disaster in history. Henceforth, ships traveled on a more southerly route in summer, when the iceberg danger was greatest. An ice patrol was established; every passenger ship had a twenty-four-hour radio watch; and from then on every ship had enough boats and life rafts for all on board.

BASEBALL
FINAL EDITION
TEMPERATURE.
Min., 46   Min., 63

The Evening Sun.

BASEBALL
FINAL EDITION
Probable showers to-night and to-mor row; warmer; E. to S. winds.

VOL. XXVI. NO. 25.   NEW YORK, MONDAY, APRIL 15, 1912.—Copyright, 1912, by The Sun Printing and Publishing Association.   PRICE ONE CENT.

ALL SAVED FROM TITANIC AFTER COLLISION

RESCUE BY CARPATHIA AND PARISIAN; LINER IS BEING TOWED TO HALIFAX AFTER SMASHING INTO AN ICEBERG

Baltic, Virginian, Olympic and Other Ships Summoned by Urgent Wireless Calls.

BIGGEST OF LINERS IN CRASH

She Carried Over 1,400 Passengers, Many of Prominence---Message from Olympic Telling of Rescue.

CANSO, N. S., April 15.—The White Star liner Titanic, having transferred her passengers to the Parisian and Carpathia, was at 2 o'clock this afternoon being towed to Halifax by the Virginian of the Allan line.

The Virginian passed a line to the Titanic as soon as the passengers had been transferred, and the latest word received by wireless was that there was no doubt that the new White Star liner would be kept afloat.

Agents of the White Star line at Halifax have been ordered to keep working tugs sent out to aid the Virginian with her tow into port.

OLYMPIC SENDS FIRST WORD OF RESCUE.

HEADS FOR HALIFAX.

Titanic Reported Afloat Limping Toward Shore.

MONTREAL, April 15.—At 8:30 o'clock an unofficial despatch reached Montreal from Halifax, stating that the Titanic was still afloat and was making her way slowly toward Halifax.

Agents of the Allan line at Halifax have no news from the Virginian. A wireless from the steamer Parisian from Glasgow states that she was 330 miles

MARCONI'S COMMENT.

Wireless Inventor Talks About Talking to Titanic.

Guglielmo Marconi, the inventor of the wireless telegraph, who is in this country at the present time, was found at the offices of the Marconi Wireless Company of America this morning, where he had gone to attend a directors' meeting. When asked about the delays in the transmission of wireless telegrams from the Titanic to-day he said that the delay was in no way due to the breaking of the

MERKLE QUITS.

Giants' First Baseman Joins Holdout Brigade.

BOSTON, April 15.—It developed here to-day that Fred Merkle, first baseman of the Giants, is a holdout. Merkle was present at the Grand Central Station in New York when John J. McGraw and the squad left for this city at midnight and refused to join the outfit. Merkle is said to want considerably more money than McGraw is willing to give him. When the team pulled out

GIANTS DROP GAME AT HUB

Boston Braves Win From McGrawites.

MATTY MAKES HIS DEBUT

Snodgrass Plays First in Place of Merkle.

BOSTON, Mass., April 15.—McGraw had to figure quickly on his line up here to-day against Johnny Kling's Boston bunch because of Merkle's defection and he called in Snodgrass from centrefield and played him on first. Becker was sent out to fill in on the centre patch. Kling had some trouble with his outfield when Jackson loomed up ill and he was forced to play Kaiser in left field in Jackson's place.

Kling, after looking over his twirling outfit, decided that Perdue should do the heavy work and in the light of this McGraw introduced Big Six Mathewson o the assembled 3,000 fans who had braved the elements to be present at the initial gathering.

Boston.	New York.
Sweeney, 2b.	Devore, l. f.
Campbell, c. f.	Doyle, 2b.
Miller, r. f.	Snodgrass, 1b.
Kaiser, l. f.	Murray, r. f.
Houser, 1b.	Becker, c. f.
Spratt, s. s.	Herzog, 3b.
McDonald, 3b.	Shafer, s. s.
Kling, c.	Meyers, c.
Perdue, p.	Mathewson, p.

Umpires—Klem and Bush. Attendance, 3,000.

FIRST INNING.

Devore out, Spratt to Houser. Doyle doubled to centre field. Snodgrass popped to Spratt. Murray fanned. No runs, one hit, no errors.

Sweeney out, Shafer to Snodgrass. Campbell flied out to Devore. Miller grounded out to Snodgrass. No runs, no hits, no errors.

SECOND INNING.

THE TITANIC UNDER WAY.

ANXIOUS INQUIRERS

from Sable Island at 8 o'clock last night, but contains no mention of the Vir-

apparatus on board the Titanic but simply that the great distance between New

Merkle was standing on the station platform bidding the other players good

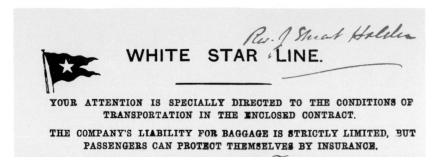

WHITE STAR LINE.

Rev. J. Stuart Holden

YOUR ATTENTION IS SPECIALLY DIRECTED TO THE CONDITIONS OF
TRANSPORTATION IN THE ENCLOSED CONTRACT.

THE COMPANY'S LIABILITY FOR BAGGAGE IS STRICTLY LIMITED, BUT
PASSENGERS CAN PROTECT THEMSELVES BY INSURANCE.

First Class Passenger Ticket per Steamship *Titanic*

SAILING FROM *14*
_____ *19*

The *Titanic* and *Olympic* were to be
White Star's entries in the luxury sweepstakes. Almost identical in size and design,
the two ships were built for comfort rather
than speed. Newsmen, noting that passage
in the deluxe suite on the *Titanic* cost
$4,350, dubbed her the "Millionaire's
Special." People clamored for tickets for her
maiden voyage. The ticket at far left was
held by a minister who canceled at the last
moment. Captain E. J. Smith (left) was at
the helm. Despite warnings like the one at
left center, which was sent by the *Amerika*,
the *Titanic* was steaming briskly along when
she hit the berg. Her radio operator sent
the world's first SOS (bottom left), adding
the old CQD—Come Quick Danger—for
good measure.

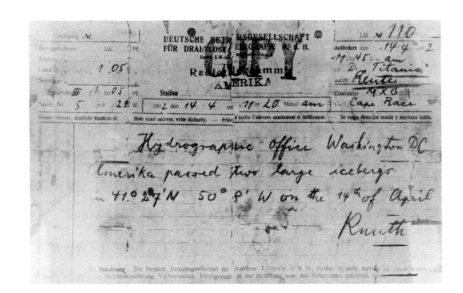

One of the many versions of the *Titanic*'s sinking (opposite) was sketched by a shocked survivor while he was sitting in a lifeboat. Contrary to the drawing, however, the ship did not split in half but went down whole, bow first, at 2:40 A.M., three hours after the collision. Captain Smith was among the casualties, as were most of the steerage passengers, who had been left to negotiate the labyrinthian passageways up to the boat deck on their own. Most did not make it, but some who almost gained the upper decks were barred from entering the first-class area. The survivors, including the terrified lifeboaters below, were mostly from first class. They were picked up (right) by Cunard's *Carpathia,* which arrived at dawn.

Aiding stunned survivors, passengers on the *Carpathia* (below) offered sympathy and warm clothing. Meanwhile, at the White Star offices in London and New York, friends, relatives, and concerned citizens were demanding to know which of the wildly circulating rumors were true. When the real dimensions of the tragedy were known, crowds raged anew seeking information about survivors. Forty thousand people lined the rainy piers of New York when the *Carpathia* arrived three days after the disaster (right, center) carrying the *Titanic*'s lifeboats (bottom right). A grateful survivor, Denver's colorful millionairess, "the unsinkable" Molly Brown, presented medals (right) to every member of the *Carpathia*'s crew.

Even before the full impact of the disaster had hit the survivors or grieving families, stories of heroism and gallantry began to surface. Mr. and Mrs. Isidor Straus (he was an owner of Macy's department store), who had posed in happier times for the photograph at right, perished together because she would not be parted from him, and he would not get into a lifeboat before any other man. The *Titanic*'s musicians, whose bravery was commemorated on the cover of the musicians' union magazine (left), played on from the moment of collision until the ship went under, only changing their tune at the end from ragtime to a final hymn. In the photograph below, the only honeymoon couple to survive the disaster consoles a new widow.

The Floating Superlatives: High Style on the Brink of War

The battle for supremacy on the North Atlantic went on unabated after the sinking of the *Titanic,* but there was a new emphasis on safety. In the two years before World War I, four new luxury liners went into service, each with its own claims to distinction.

The 1912 *France,* arriving in New York barely a month after the *Titanic* went down, was the smallest but probably the most elegant of the four. "You are in France the moment you cross the gangplank," crooned the publicists for the Compagnie Générale Transatlantique.

Size and comfort were the goals for Hamburg–America's *Imperator* and *Vaterland,* Germany's first big turbine liners, which entered service in 1913 and 1914 respectively. The *Imperator* alone carried 5,500 passengers and crew. The biggest ships in the world when they were launched, they were the first of a trio of giants with which Hamburg–America hoped to inaugurate a weekly service to New York. The third giant, the *Bismarck,* was still on the stocks when the war broke out.

The *Aquitania* (1914) was designed to be the running mate of the *Mauretania* and *Lusitania.* Named for a Roman province in southern France, she was an anthology of European culture, with rooms of every style and period.

FRANCE
HAVRE

Down the ways they came, one quintessential liner after another, as the grab for passenger dollars became more intense. The *Aquitania,* seen steaming through heavy seas (opposite), was launched amid a Cunard chorus of mosts, biggests, and bests. But she was smaller than Hamburg–America's *Imperator* (left) and *Vaterland* (below), the latter being just over nine hundred feet long, which made her the biggest thing afloat. The *Vaterland* was more stable than the *Imperator,* which was notoriciusly top-heavy and rolled sickeningly even in the calmest weather (see photo at left). The French Line, unable to compete in size with the British and German liners, intended the *France* (far left) to overwhelm with Gallic luxuries.

The *Imperator* was fitted out to be the grandest ship afloat. Charles Mewès stopped at nothing in decorating the new leviathan. The ornamental staircase (below), adorned with a portrait of the Kaiser, provided an elegant setting for a stately progress between decks (or a good slide for little boys)—although by now elevators were a standard feature aboard all luxury liners. Aboard the *Imperator,* too, those who were fond of athletics could choose between the Mewès' extraordinary "Pompeian Bath" (right), which was the twin of a bath he had designed for London's Royal Automobile Club; or the well-equipped gymnasium (right, below) where the vigilant instructor kept a watchful eye out for slackers.

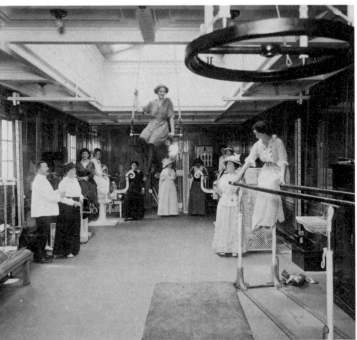

The *Aquitania,* boasting all the elegance the average millionaire could handle, also carried a deckful of lifeboats (below, right) and another new twist. A British newspaper reported: "Aquitania has no steerage. Instead she has a third-class cabin. . . . It must not be supposed that [it] provides all the luxuries that a fastidious tourist desires, but in this instance it is so far above the sodden human welter of the old steerage that it deserves to be welcomed." Attention on the *France* centered on the dining room (below) and the cuisine. She began each crossing with eighteen barrels of pâté and the freshest viands in her galleys. In the dome-lit grand saloon (top, right) Louis XIV dominates the scene.

The bows of Germany's two prewar giants, the *Vaterland* (below) and the *Imperator* (left, below), sported appropriately imperial decorations. The *Imperator*'s huge cast iron eagle, which clutched in its talons a globe bearing Hamburg–America's motto, Mien Feld Ist die Welt (My Field is the World), added ten feet to the ship's length, making it temporarily the world's longest liner. But the device also aggravated the ship's top-heaviness. During the ship's third crossing, a storm wrenched the bird off the bow. The owners took the hint. The eagle was not replaced; and to help make the *Imperator* more stable the ship's funnels were cut down, and many of her mahogany and marble decorations were replaced with wallpaper, and tile.

Deepening European hostilities were in the background during the festive launch ceremonies of the *Vaterland* and *Imperator*, and yet there was a certain militaristic ambiance. Kaiser Wilhelm II, dressed as an admiral to christen the *Imperator* (seen below, atop the tower), was watched by a crowd that was dotted with helmets. At right, Prince Rupert accompanies the *Vaterland*'s builders in a stroll around the ship's enormous hull. The smiling man behind the Prince is Albert Ballin. What satisfaction the two men—and the rest of Germany—may have enjoyed at the launch of the mighty ships was to be short-lived, for both the *Vaterland* and the *Imperator* would soon be making their last runs under the German flag.

Liners at War

1914–1918

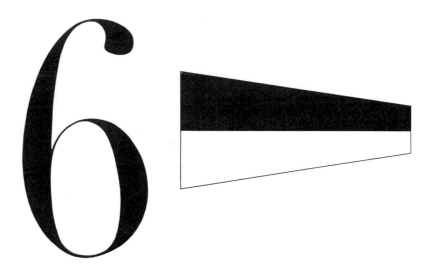

The Great War begins in Europe, and British and German liners race for cover, having suddenly become fair game for belligerent warships. . . . Fitted with guns and armor plate, some liners wear the dress of battle cruisers. . . . Others, despite the danger of attack, continue plying the passenger trade . . . until the *Lusitania*, running the gauntlet once too often, is torpedoed and sunk by a German submarine. . . . Meanwhile, in the rush for fresh troops and passage for the wounded, many liners find their true vocation as troop transports and hospital ships, carrying millions of men off to war . . . and bringing the fortunate ones home again.

Battling it out, Cunard's *Carmania* (foreground) takes a pounding from Hamburg–South America's *Cap Trafalgar*, herself mortally wounded by the *Carmania's* guns. The encounter is shown here in a painting by an eyewitness.

"Urgent and Confidential: Erhard has
suffered attack of catarrh of the bladder.
Siegfried."

—CODED MESSAGE WARNING GERMAN LINERS OF
IMPENDING WAR, JULY 31, 1914

A crackling of wireless messages marked the start of World War I on the North Atlantic. In the last days of July and the first of August, 1914, the big liners, warned by radio of the outbreak of hostilities, raced to take cover in the nearest friendly port.

The *Mauretania,* bound for New York, dimmed her lights, cut off all communications, and dashed through the fog to Halifax. The *Olympic* stayed on course for New York, running at full speed. The *Lusitania* and the French Line's *La Lorraine* slipped out of New York within hours of the British declaration of war. Anxious to get home, their captains decided to trust to speed for a safe crossing. Rumors reported the ships were captured and destroyed, but both made it across without incident.

Meanwhile, Germany's *Kronprinzessen Cecilie,* bound for Bremerhaven with some $12 million in bullion on board, sailed back into American waters as fast as she could. She put in at the small resort town of Bar Harbor, Maine—a great, black-hulled presence among the vacationers' yachts and canoes.

More than thirty German ships were caught in United States ports, their exits blocked by patrolling British warships. Several tried to make a run for it but had to turn back. The *Friedrich der Grosse,* two days out of Baltimore, turned around after having

narrowly escaped a British cruiser. Others followed her lead and prepared for a long stay. Among the trapped was the *Vaterland,* Germany's newest ship and the world's largest. She was laid up in Hoboken, New Jersey, in the midst of her fourth voyage. Her running mate, the *Imperator,* was tied up in Hamburg, where she remained for the duration of the war. In the confusion that resulted when so many schedules were disrupted, thousands of Americans found themselves stranded in Europe, and they had to get home by whatever ships were available.

That the big, speedy Atlantic liners might double as warships had long been a pet idea of both the German and British admiralties. Both navies had spent huge sums of money subsidizing the big liners, with the understanding that the ships would be commandeered in an emergency. (It was such a subsidy that helped save Cunard from falling into the hands of J. P. Morgan in 1903.)

Now that the emergency had become a reality the transition was swift. Germany's *Kronprinz Wilhelm* and the *Cap Trafalgar* (of the Hamburg–South American Line) were armed at sea in the very first days of the war. In Halifax, guns began to appear on the decks of the *Mauretania* even before the last passenger had debarked for the train to New York.

Unfortunately for the naval theorists, the big liners proved to be expensive disappointments as fighters. In the first place, their hulls and superstructures were not designed for war and were terribly vulnerable. In the single sea battle fought between armed merchantmen during the entire war, Cunard's *Carmania* and the *Cap Trafalgar* met off the island of Trinidad, seven hundred miles east of Rio de Janeiro, in mid-September, 1914. The two were about equal in size and speed. But while the German gunners made a shambles of the *Carmania*'s bridge and decks, the British crew concentrated their fire on the *Cap Trafalgar*'s waterline, causing the German ship to finally capsize and sink.

Amateur gunners and weak superstructures only mattered, however, when the liners could afford to put to sea, which the biggest liners could not do. Because they burned so much coal, they were simply too expensive to operate effectively as cruisers. The *Mauretania,* for one, spent the first years of the war tied up at her pier, since the Admiralty could not afford to keep her bunkers full.

Another problem became apparent with the wartime career of the *Kaiser Wilhelm der Grosse,* a career lasting all of three weeks. During that time, the liner did manage to sink a couple of freighters.

The array of liners detained at Hoboken in 1914 (left) constituted a substantial portion of the German passenger fleet. Included was the *Vaterland* at left and the *Kaiser Wilhelm* and *George Washington* at far right. When the war began, more than ninety German vessels were held in neutral ports. The Germans captured some eighty British ships but failed to trap a single major carrier among them. The photo below shows the deck and bridge of the *Carmania* as they looked after the Cunarder was armed with eight 4.7-inch guns. In her winning battle with Germany's *Cap Trafalgar,* the *Carmania's* superstructure was badly riddled; below left, is a close-up of one hit in her inadequate armor plating.

But Germany's first record-breaker was herself sunk when an old, worn-out British cruiser discovered her coaling up off the coast of West Africa. Although the *Wilhelm* was certainly faster at sea than her attacker, she was a sitting duck when tied by her heels to the coal boats.

Coaling at sea made the big liners extremely vulnerable, but there was no alternative since they were too big to enter most ports of refuge. Nor could they get the regular end-of-voyage maintenance they needed to keep in trim. The *Kronprinz Wilhelm,* for instance, having used the arms she took aboard in the West Indies to sink eight ships in as many months, finally had to call it quits; with her bunkers almost empty and her engines all but unusable, she came limping into Newport News, Virginia, and was promptly interned.

If the big liners failed to earn their subsidies as warships, however, they were to perform magnificently when called upon to do service as troop transports and hospital ships. It was, after all, the job they were designed for: ferrying large numbers of people over the sea in the shortest possible time. Operating on the Mediterranean as well as the North Atlantic, they were to play an invaluable role in the Allied war effort.

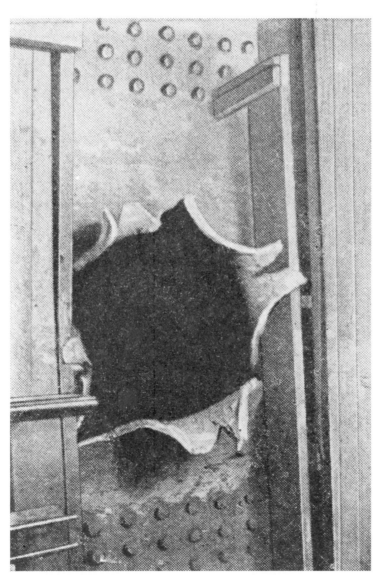

Having found refuge in a neutral port, Germany's *Kronprinzessen Cecilie* lies at anchor off Bar Harbor, Maine (left and below), where her officers were soon being lionized at society balls and parties. During her dash for cover, the tops of her yellow funnels had been painted black to make her look like White Star's *Olympic;* but the pairing of her funnels would have been a dead giveaway had she been spotted by the Royal Navy. At right, a contingent of police guards a fleet of German liners interned in New York. Having escaped capture by British warships, these vessels, like the *Cecilie,* were seized by the United States when it entered the war and were converted for use as American troop carriers and transports.

The interned liners *Kronprinz Wilhelm* and *Prinz Eitel Friedrich* ride quietly at anchor near Newport News, Virginia (left), where crew members (below) march to barracks prepared for them by U.S. officials. About half the personnel from detained ships sat out the war in U.S. custody. Others managed to return to Germany, while some simply melted into the American scene. In most cases, those who stayed behind remained on board their ships performing maintenance chores. Until the United States entered the war, they were free to visit friends and even to raise money for the German war effort. Still, boredom was a problem, and officers found strict shipboard discipline impossible to maintain. On the opposite page, German seamen interned in Newport News, Virginia, take time to pose for a group portrait (top); another photo (lower right) shows a seaman standing guard on his idle ship. The ships' bands, like the one at the bottom, often entertained town residents as well as their own mates. At Norfolk, the German seamen led a fairly regular life. They even constructed a miniature German city for themselves, complete with gaily painted houses, a miniature farm, a school, a gymnasium, and a police and fire department. Thousands of visitors paid ten cents each to see the town, and they were treated to a program of athletic exhibitions and a copy of the pro-German newspaper which was published by the crewmen.

The *Lusitania:* "Liable to Destruction"

The usual festive spirit of a departure was missing when passengers boarded the *Lusitania* in New York on May 1, 1915. Everyone was too nervous. That morning the newspapers had carried a warning from the Imperial German Embassy in Washington declaring that British vessels were "liable to destruction," and that Americans sailed on them at their own risk.

The *Lusitania's* captain, however, assured his worried passengers that there was little to fear. He said his ship was quite fast enough to outrun any submarine, and besides, she was to have the protection of a cruiser escort once she entered the European war zone. Thus, she sailed on schedule, with nearly two thousand souls aboard.

The *Lusitania* was the only large liner still operating on the North Atlantic, making a monthly voyage between Liverpool and New York. Most of Germany's merchant fleet had been blockaded in German and American ports; while the rest of Britain's giant liners were doing service as cruisers, transports, or hospital ships.

The shortage of vessels, meanwhile, along with the upheaval of war, had severely reduced business and pleasure travel between Europe and America, and emigration had fallen off precipitously. What traffic there was traveled mostly on neutral ships, bringing huge profits to lines like Holland–America, Swedish–American, and America's International Mercantile Marine.

But Cunard and White Star were doing their best to maintain a regular transatlantic service. To most people the idea that peaceful travelers were liable to attack was simply beyond imagining.

All that changed at noontime on May 7, 1915, when the *Lusitania* was torpedoed off the southern coast of Ireland. Her cruiser escort had failed to appear, despite the fact that submarines were known to be in the area. Diverted to Queenstown and already within sight of land, she ran straight across the path of a lurking U-boat. Struck by a single torpedo just forward of the bridge on her starboard side, she was immediately torn by a second explosion, apparently of contraband munitions, that blew out most of the bottom of the bow. She sank within twenty minutes, with a loss of some twelve hundred lives, 128 of them Americans.

Whether or not—as some have suggested—the *Lusitania* was deliberately served up as "live bait" in order to hasten America's entry into the war, the effect was the same. The sinking turned America's sympathies decisively against the German cause.

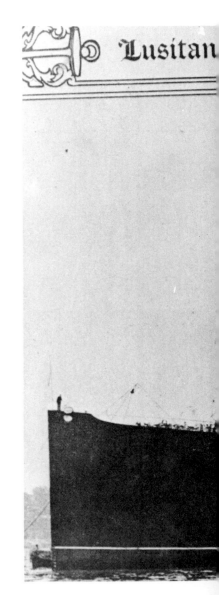

Spelling out disaster, a newspaper head-
line (below) is accompanied by a picture
of the *Lusitania* in less frightful times. For
the great ship, a prewar departure (like
that shown in the photograph below, right)
had been a relaxed and happy affair, but
wartime travelers crossed only out of
necessity. When the *Lusitania* sailed for
the last time, all were apprehensive due to
the warning from the German Embassy that
had been published in eerie juxtaposition
with a *Lusitania* advertisement (opposite).
After the ship was torpedoed, Captain
William Turner, shown on the bridge
just before the last sailing (right), was
blamed for not zigzagging in waters known
to be infested with U-boats. The sinking
plagued him for the rest of his life.

Once Queen of the Seas, Destroyed by Germans May 7

IRISH COAST - Cork County

STERN BRIDGE

2nd Class Quarters

Palm Lounge

CORK

QUEENSTOWN
from which
assistance was
despatched

KINSALE
first Boats despatched

Roches Point
entrance to
Cork Harbour

Daunt's
Rock

Lighthouse on
Old Head of Kinsale.
Keeper telephones
to Kinsale

Distance from Liner
to Headland, 8 miles

Trawlers which
rendered assistance

Bow becoming
submerged

Captains
Bridge

Wireless
Cabin

rition
t Class
ng
oon

The *Lusitania*'s sinking is depicted in these drawings from an English weekly of May, 1915. As the paper explained, a man (opposite) "looking out to sea suddenly perceived a white streak close to the surface. . . . He cried, 'Look out! There's a torpedo coming,' and they all watched its progress." The perspective drawing at left shows the ship's position relative to the Irish coast; while below, people struggle to get away from the listing ship. Only six of forty-eight lifeboats made land. Starboard boats swung out so far that they were dangerous to enter. Most lifeboats on the high port side were useless because of the ship's list. Many crashed to the water. The others hurtled toward the bow, crushing people along the way.

Thousands from all over Ireland gathered at the mass funeral for the victims of the *Lusitania* tragedy (left). The English medal below was copied from a German version that was mistakenly believed to celebrate the sinking of the liner. Nevertheless, it served its purpose of provoking anti-German sentiment. Similarly, the evocative nature of the podium (below) was a great help to army recruiters and to speakers who were raising money for the war effort. The lifejacket (right) was found floating near Philadelphia. Opposite right, the Hunnish "Excuse Me" being offered to a grim Uncle Sam appeared in a May, 1915, *Literary Digest*. The torrent of publicity that followed the sinking turned America against Germany.

"Over There" and Back in Converted Luxury

It was as troop carriers and hospital ships that the big liners did their best wartime service. Canadian liners provided the war's first large-scale movement of men and supplies; while British and French liners—notably the *Aquitania, Mauretania, Olympic,* and *France*—saw service both in the Mediterranean and on the North Atlantic. The major casualty was the brand-new *Britannic,* third of White Star's *Olympic*-class liners. Fitted out as a hospital ship, she struck a mine and sank in the Aegean in 1916. Twenty-eight lives were lost but it could have been worse; there were 1,100 aboard at the time.

Once the United States entered the war in 1917, the big German liners that had been sitting in American ports since the start of hostilities provided the United States with a ready-made fleet of speedy troopers and supply ships. It was "the fleet the Kaiser built for us," and it included some of the biggest and most elegant liners of the day. The most valuable prize of all was the *Vaterland.* Rechristened *Leviathan,* she was at that time the largest ship in the world. When her steerage and class accommodations were redone, she could carry as many as fourteen thousand men "over there" on each crossing. Together with other allied transports, she helped to carry some two million men across to France.

CHAS. PEARS. 1917.

The spectacular displays of "dazzle painting" that adorned Allied troopships during World War I were designed to break up the horizontal and vertical lines of the ships. The hope was that a submarine captain would mistake his quarry's direction and the position of its vital parts. The *Leviathan* (above) came out looking like an enormous seagoing predator. The *Empress of Russia* (right) sported a rakish bow design. The sweeping curves painted on the side of the *Olympic* (at top, opposite) dwarf the smaller ship lying alongside; while a detail of the *Mauretania*'s check-bedecked hull appears below, opposite. As dazzling as the camouflage scheme was, however, there is no evidence that it ever foiled an attack.

Like passengers for generations, troops sought ways to break the monotony of an Atlantic crossing. Boxing matches, like the one shown in the photograph above (left), always brought out a good crowd, as did the traditional shipboard competition of a three-legged race (above). Dancing was not quite as popular as with peacetime travelers since the proportion of male to female dancing partners was not what it might have been, but that didn't stop the more determined and lightfooted servicemen, like those above (center). Meanwhile, crowded quarters, third-class food, and seasickness could make a crossing pretty miserable. One regulation stated flatly that "men vomiting on the deck should be made to clean it up. . . . It is a mean trick to vomit in the home of others." How well the rule was enforced is not known, but it is some indication of conditions on board that the rule had to be issued at all.

Having gotten the doughboys to the war zone—those below (left) are disembarking from the *Leviathan* at Brest—the great liner-transports were ready to carry the sick and wounded back home again. The huge public rooms of the *Leviathan* (bottom left) served as hospital wards for Americans; while the elegant lounge inspired by Charles Mewès for the *Aquitania* (below) provided splendid accommodations for those wounded in Britain's disastrous Dardanelles campaign. Hospital ships were usually painted white with large red crosses and were girdled by a lighted red band to warn off submarines. But the worst disaster to hit a trooper or hospital ship resulted from a flu epidemic that killed ninety-six aboard the *Leviathan*.

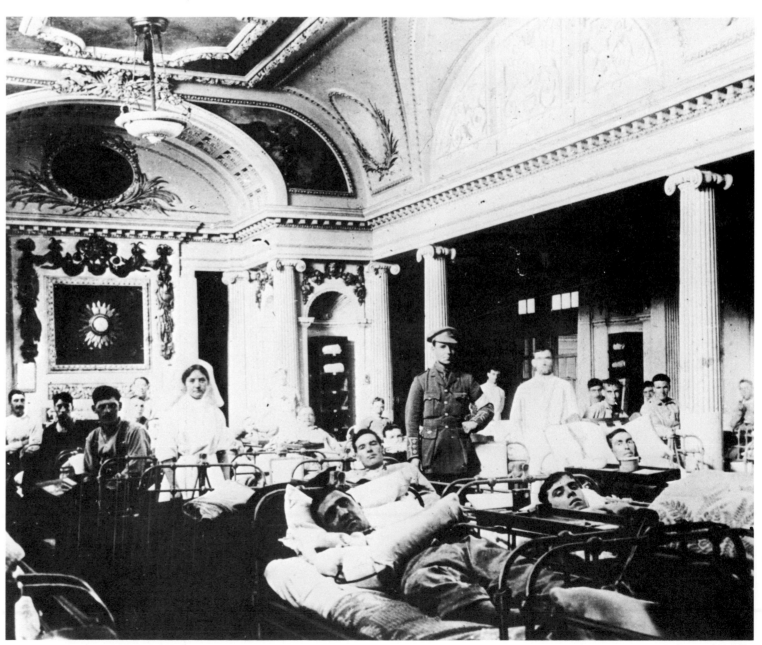

With the armistice signed and millions of American and Canadian soldiers eager to return home, the Atlantic liners embarked on their last wartime mission. Loaded to the gunwales with returning veterans, the *Leviathan* (above) was nudged up to her New York pier, where thousands of people came to cheer her arrival. Relatives and friends had to jockey for a place among politicians, bands, reporters, the police glee club, and a two-hundred-member welcoming committee. The flag-waving throng at top (right) greeted the *Mauretania* when she pulled into Manhattan with her precious cargo. But it was a subdued crowd that awaited the docking of the hospital ship *France* (right), which was bringing wounded Americans home.

Getting their first close-up look at America since they sailed off to war, troops aboard the returning *Leviathan* (below) and *Mauretania* (right) crowd every available vantage point, including ventilators and lifeboats. Although regular transatlantic service was restored in 1919, for many months after the war almost all passenger space on British and American ships was given over to ferrying Canadian and American military personnel home. After that it took still more time to remove the bunks and mess tables, to replace the paintings and the potted palms, and to repaint the ships inside and out.

Champagne and Caviar

1919–1929

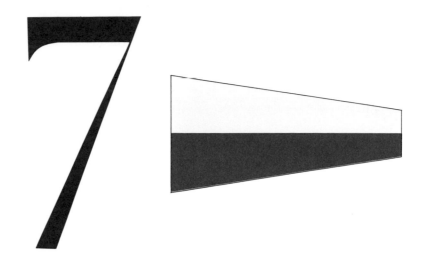

In the aftermath of war, the liners that survive are dressed once more in civilian colors . . . and the great German ships, seized as war prizes, now fly the flags of Britain and America. . . . Gradually, elegance and luxury return on the North Atlantic run . . . tourist third replaces emigrant steerage on most big liners . . . and a dashing newcomer, the *Ile de France*, emerges as the prestige liner of the twenties. . . . It is the era of glamorous midnight sailings, of miniature golf, dancing in the dark, and bouillon after breakfast. . . . The Atlantic liner, no longer just a means of getting to and from somewhere, is now a place to be: a world all its own.

Lights dimmed, club chairs pushed back, the grand saloon of the *Ile de France* was transformed nightly into a sumptuous ballroom—where the environment was, according to the ship's publicists, "so assuredly correct."

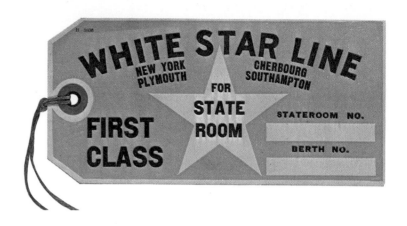

To the seasoned traveler the scene would have been familiar: the cabins were being made ready; the steamer trunks, plastered with stickers, were being carried below; and at the rail, passengers were shouting farewells to friends ashore. The war was over. The big liners, their camouflage painted over and the guns removed from their decks, were casting off once more on the North Atlantic run.

Despite the familiarity of the scene, however, there had been many changes since the prewar years. For one thing, the flags of Hamburg–America and the North German Lloyd, previously among the most common, were now rarely seen. The victorious Allies had stripped Germany of practically every ship in its merchant fleet. Foremost among the war prizes were Hamburg–America's big three: the *Vaterland,* the *Imperator,* and the *Bismarck,* which would remain the largest ships afloat until the *Normandie* appeared in 1935.

The *Leviathan* (ex–*Vaterland*), now embarked on a career as the queen of the United States commercial fleet, began her maiden voyage on July 4th, 1923. The *Imperator,* replacing Cunard's *Lusitania,* had her funnels painted red and black, her Ritz-Carlton restaurant converted to a ballroom, and her name changed to *Berengaria,* after the wife of Richard

the Lion-Hearted. The *Bismarck,* launched just before the war, completed her fitting out in German and British shipyards, was renamed *Majestic,* and entered service in 1922.

Another change of the postwar years, the conversion of most of the big liners from coal to oil, would have become apparent to the traveler in the hours just before sailing. Gone was the sound of coal thundering down the chutes into the bunkers; and gone were the layers of coal dust that had coated the railings, portholes, and deck chairs after a ship had been bunkered up.

But it was economics not aesthetics that prompted the changeover. Although oil was still more expensive than coal, it gave more heat energy, required less storage space, and could be loaded faster, thus reducing the time a ship had to spend idle in port. But perhaps the most significant savings for the companies came from the fact that the stokehole crew could be drastically reduced—from 350 men to 50 in the case of the *Aquitania.*

Meantime, as the liners themselves were changing, so were the kind and number of people who traveled on them. The big shift came as a result of America's restrictive Quota Act of 1921. Known as the Three Percent Act, it restricted immigration to three per-

cent of each nationality already residing in America, based on the 1903 census. Immediately the number of people sailing westward from Europe declined sharply. This was bad news for the giant ocean liners, which had been built to transport a thousand and more steerage passengers on each crossing.

What saved the liners was a whole new class of traveler: the American tourist, who wanted to see the sights and absorb the culture of Europe as cheaply as possible. This new source of steamship revenue was first recognized, it seems, by a branch manager of the International Mercantile Marine, a Mr. L. S. Tobin. Converting the steerage facilities of International Mercantile Marine's *Regina* to "tourist third class," Tobin offered an inexpensive trip to Europe for students, teachers, and anyone else who cared to share the adventure but could only afford the minimum fare. With 537 passengers of this new class aboard, the *Regina* left on the first so-called College Tour in June, 1924.

The idea quickly caught fire, with one steamship line after another converting its steerage space to tourist third. Typically this meant a cramped little cabin shared with strangers, a passable menu, and towels that bore the company monogram. It was all very bohemian—and very popular.

With each sailing a formidable assortment of luggage, such as crowds the deck below, had to be sorted. Travel in the stylish twenties required an elaborate wardrobe solely for wear during the voyage, and it was common practice to pack a separate steamer trunk, which was set up in the cabin like a portable chest of drawers. On arrival in Europe the steamship companies obligingly stored these trunks free of charge while their owners toured, accompanied now by luggage from the hold. A traveler's total suite of luggage might amount to scores of pieces, and distinctive luggage tags, like those at left and right, not only helped to keep confusion to a minimum, but also gave one's luggage a certain panache.

Americans, it turned out, were immensely curious about Europe. They were also thirsty, and once outside United States territorial waters they could drink when, what, and where they pleased, provided they were sailing on a foreign ship. (Prohibition was one reason why the *Leviathan* never made a profit; another was that she had no fast running mates to keep up a regular and frequent express service.)

Enjoying a newfound, if sometimes moderate prosperity, Americans made the trip to Europe in astonishingly large numbers. In 1927, North Atlantic passengers exceeded the one million mark for the first time since the prewar emigration years; and fully 80 percent of those million were Americans.

Not all of this traffic was tourist class, of course. On the contrary, first-class elegance and glamour set the tone of the decade. The ship that epitomized the new era—modern, racy, and romantic—was the famed *Ile de France*. Designed after the Quota Act had stemmed the tide of emigration, she was intended first and foremost for the luxury trade. Making her maiden voyage in 1927, she was an immediate and huge success, proving beyond a doubt that luxury liners could still pay their way. She proved it so well that by the end of the decade a new bout of Blue Ribbon fever was under way.

With the bulk of passenger lists now made up of Americans, North Atlantic steamship companies waged an active advertising campaign for business. The result was often as appealing to the eye as it was productive for the companies, as witness these lavish posters: from left, Cunard's war veteran *Aquitania,* now dressed in civilian colors; Norwegian–America's *Stavangerfjord,* launched in 1918; Swedish–American's *Drottningholm* of 1905; White Star's German war prize, the *Majestic* (ex–*Bismarck*), which, at 915 feet, was the longest ship then in service; Red Star's *Belgenland,* in service from 1923; Holland–America's *Statendam;* and the French Line's glamour ship *Paris,* launched in 1916 but not in commercial service until 1921. The *Paris* remained the flagship of France's postwar fleet until 1927, when the ultra-chic *Ile de France* appeared. At far right is a publicity brochure designed to tempt travelers to go first class aboard the *Ile de France.*

Baggage, Bouquets, and Bon Voyage

What gripped most passengers instantly upon crossing the gangplank was the sense of make-believe of a ship, a certain aura of surreal rituals being performed, seen and unseen, all around, that made this world not like anything else they knew.

Rituals gave some order to the exciting but vaguely unsettling experience of crossing three thousand miles of ocean in what one writer called "a floating iron eggshell." The bon voyage party, which originated in the days when travel was no pleasure and good-byes were all too likely to be permanent, helped now to make the transition to the unreal realities of shipboard life.

Once at sea, the first order of business for some was unpacking the baggage and getting settled in the cabin. For others, it was a tour round the ship. In any case, the anxiety and excitement of a departure did not die quickly. Sinclair Lewis conveyed the wonder of it all when he described the fictional departure for Europe of Samuel Dodsworth, his quintessential American business tycoon: "He looked along the sweep of the gangways, past the huge lifeboats, the ventilators like giant saxophones, past the lofty funnels serenely dribbling black woolly smoke, to the forward mast. . . . He was pricked to imaginativeness. . . . 'I'm at sea!' "

The ritual of departure began at the pier where officers and baggage attendants oversaw the loading of luggage, as in the photo opposite, taken before a sailing of the *Mauretania*. Also opposite is the gallant lady herself, garlanded with lights for a midnight sailing from Cherbourg. Daytime departures called for paper streamers. Supplied to passengers and stay-behinds alike, they helped make the occasion as festive as a wedding. The shower above accompanied a sailing of the *Franconia*. And always there were the obligatory good-bye gestures from ship-side, as at right, aboard the *Carmania*. The drawing opposite (bottom) and similar sketches appearing in this chapter are from Cunard and French Line brochures.

The hours before sailing had a rhythm all their own, whether one lived them as a member of the crew or as a passenger. In the photograph opposite, left, a stewardess and two stewards put the last spit and polish on the Imperial Suite of the *Berengaria*. Opposite below, cabin boys sort out bon voyage gifts; flowers and heaping fruit baskets, perhaps a holdover from the days when travelers on long voyages risked scurvy, were the conventional tributes. Meanwhile, passengers and guests took the obligatory tour of the ship's public rooms: the monumental staircase (opposite, top) was the main thoroughfare for first-class passengers aboard the *Ile de France*. Parties, which in the twenties usually meant dances, were provided as a grand send-off, an excellent bit of public relations that left shore-bound well-wishers (potential clients, after all) with a bittersweet taste of what fun a voyage could be. At right, bon voyage celebrants fox-trot aboard the *Mauretania*.

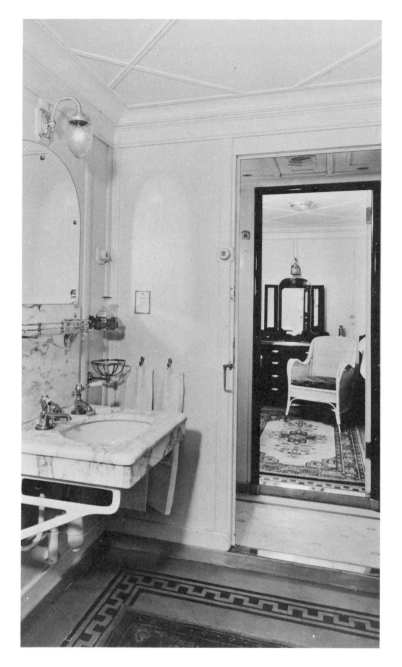

Getting settled in one's stateroom was best accomplished—in first class, at least—with the help of one's valet or maid, as in the drawing above, from a brochure promoting the French Line's *De Grasse*. The *Berengaria*'s Imperial Suite (opposite) was a notable example of what one critic called "hotelism . . . a sort of artistic hydrophobia in that those responsible for the interior decoration of a modern liner are mortally afraid to leave an indication that the scenes of their efforts belong to an oceangoing vessel." By 1929, when the *Statendam* ran her maiden voyage, small but separate washroom facilities (left) had become a feature in first class. Rather less elegant was the third-class cabin (right) aboard the *Albert Ballin*.

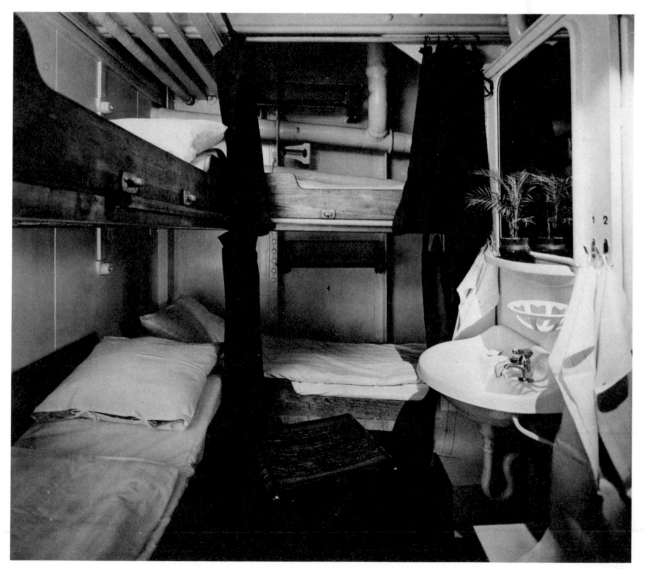

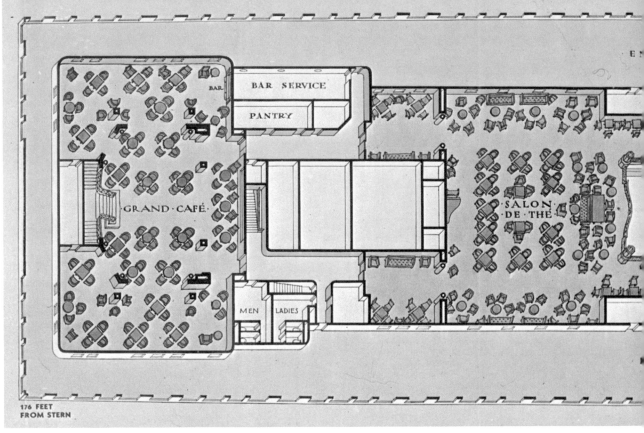

176 FEET
FROM STERN

Just sixty-three years to the day after the French Line's 3500-ton clipper-rigged and paddle-powered *Washington* hove into New York Harbor to inaugurate the Compagnie Générale Transatlantique's France–America service, the stately *Ile de France* (above) arrived on her maiden voyage. Three red and black stacks (two real and the third a ventilator in disguise) gave her a distinctive profile, but what really set her apart was her reputation, almost instantly achieved, for providing the very best in Gallic luxury.

The plan of the promenade deck (top right) shows some of the spacious public rooms reserved to the 670 first-class passengers—including the grande café, a combination *fumoir,* bar, and cabaret aft; a marble-clad grand staircase that swept all the way down to C Deck, amidships (see photo, page 178); and a *grande salle* or drawing room, forward. A few first-class cabins were located on the promenade deck, but the very best accommodations were to be found on A deck (bottom, right), including one grand-luxe suite (#263), eight deluxe, and several dozen conventional first-class accommodations.

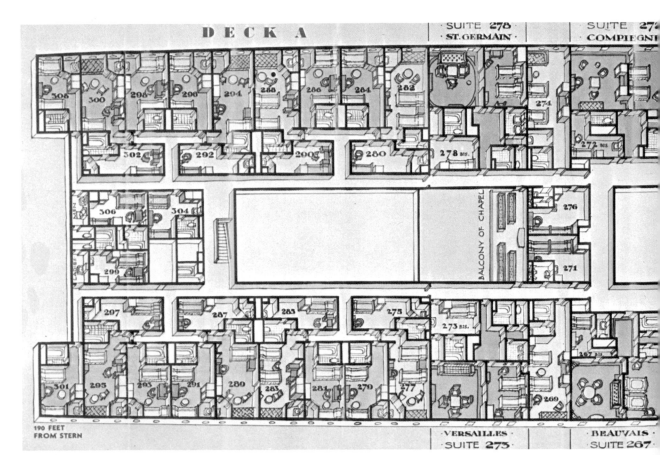

DECK A

SUITE 278
ST. GERMAIN

SUITE 27
COMPIEGNI

190 FEET
FROM STERN

VERSAILLES
SUITE 273

BEAUVAIS
SUITE 267

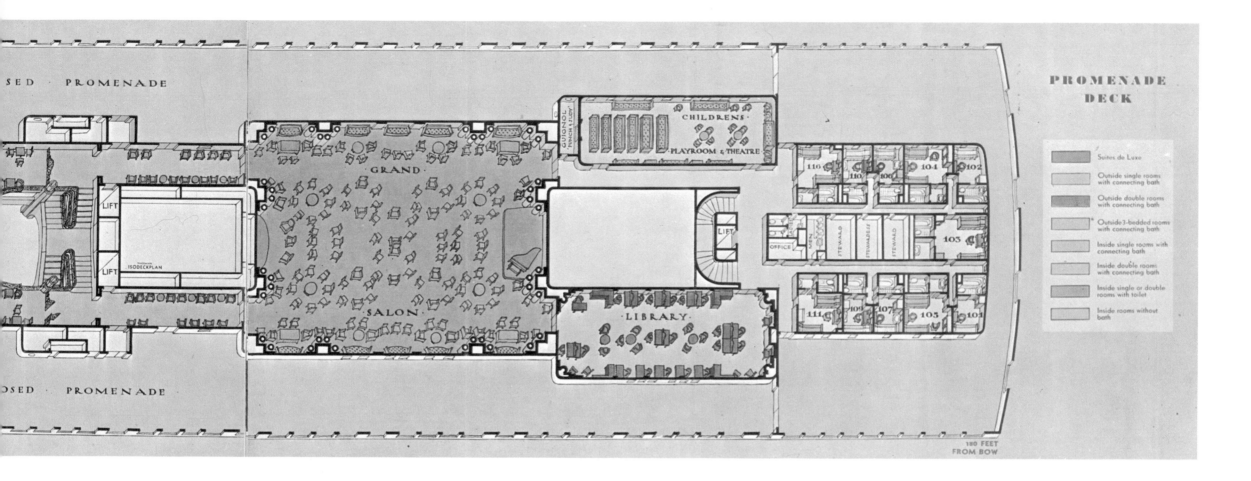

PROMENADE DECK

GRAND SALON

CHILDRENS PLAYROOM & THEATRE

LIBRARY

GUIGNOL

LIFT

LIFT

LIFT

OFFICE   MEN   STEWARD   STEWARDESS   STEWARD

116   110   106   104   102

105

111   109   107   105   101

ENCLOSED PROMENADE

ENCLOSED PROMENADE

ISODECKPLAN

Suites de Luxe

Outside single rooms with connecting bath

Outside double rooms with connecting bath

Outside 3-bedded rooms with connecting bath

Inside single rooms with connecting bath

Inside double rooms with connecting bath

Inside single or double rooms with toilet

Inside rooms without bath

180 FEET FROM BOW

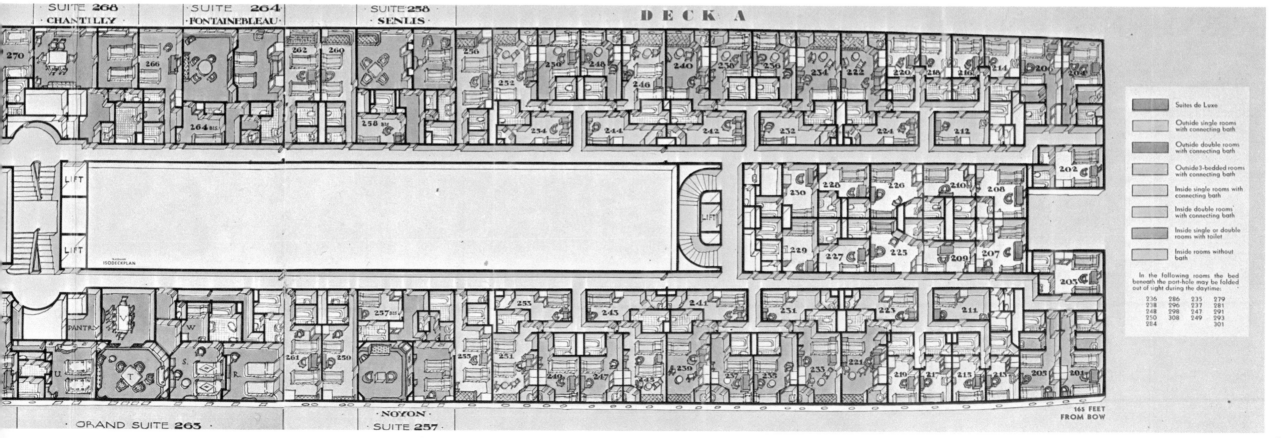

DECK A

SUITE 268 CHANTILLY   SUITE 264 FONTAINEBLEAU   SUITE 258 SENLIS

270   266   262   260   256   250   248   240   238   236   234   222   220   218   216   214   206   204

264 BIS   258 BIS   252   246   230   202

254   244   242   232   224   212

LIFT   LIFT   ISODECKPLAN   230   228   226   210   208   202

229   227   225   209   207   205

PANTRY   261   259   257 BIS   253   243   241   251   231   223   211

261   259   253   251   249   247   239   233   221   210   217   215   205   201

GRAND SUITE 263   NOYON SUITE 257

Suites de Luxe

Outside single rooms with connecting bath

Outside double rooms with connecting bath

Outside 3-bedded rooms with connecting bath

Inside single rooms with connecting bath

Inside double rooms with connecting bath

Inside single or double room with toilet

Inside rooms without bath

In the following rooms the bed beneath the port-hole may be folded out of sight during the daytime:

236	286	235	279
238	296	237	281
248	298	247	291
250	308	249	293
284			301

165 FEET FROM BOW

183

Chatting, strolling, and an alternating
succession of refreshment breaks made the
hours pass quickly. Opposite (top), a
sporting group savors a bracing cup of
bouillon. Also opposite (center row), one
of the smart set sips tea in the *Statendam*'s
verandah café and French-speaking cabin
boys learn to respond in English to an
often-asked question. Opposite right, two
well-dressed matrons and their borzoi visit
the shuffleboard scene. Meanwhile, the
ship's officers take time out to pose for
photos: among the gauges and controls of
the engine room (below, aboard the
Majestic) and on deck with their sextants
(left). Despite the sophisticated technology
of the modern liner, the sextant was still
used for checking a ship's position.

Rites of Passage

A day at sea for most passengers was a pleasant
exercise in indolence. However firmly a voyager might
resolve to catch up on his reading or to carry out
some other self-improvement project, everything
about seaborne life conspired to distract him from
serious pursuits. A brochure, describing the allure-
ments of the French Line's *Paris,* offered the
following advice: "Play and the world plays with
you. . . . Games on shipboard give you just enough
healthful exercise and spontaneous laughter to
prepare you thoroughly to enjoy the many other
diversions of the day."

Some of these diversions could be enjoyed from a
deck chair reserved for the length of the voyage,
and the seasoned traveler made every effort to see
that his topside neighbors were at least as congenial
and socially well-placed as his dining room table
mates. The deck steward, who orchestrated fresh air
seating arrangements, found himself in a position of
of considerable power. But the deck chair was just
a base of social operation. Promenading was the way
to see and be seen. A brochure advertising the merits
of the *France* burbled that a stroll around the
promenade deck was "the World's best make-up
box. Once around—rouge. Twice around—eyes that
laugh and challenge. Three times—youth."

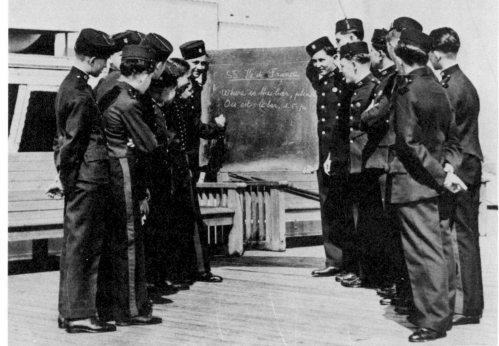

Where the Elite Meet in Twenties' Style

Eddie and Ida Cantor and the Ziegfeld Girls

The Winston Churchills and daughter Diana

Charlie Chaplin

Golf great Bobby Jones

J. P. Morgan, Jr.

Rudolph Valentino and Sophie Tucker

Dorothy Thompson and Sinclair Lewis

Mme Marie Curie

Fred and Adele Astaire

Gertrude Stein and Alice B. Toklas

Jack Dempsey

Tom Mix and his horse Tony

F. Scott Fitzgerald and daughter Scotty

Pavlova and the Ballet Russe corps de ballet

Bill Tilden (third from left) and the Davis Cup Tennis Team, 1928

Lady Astor

Sir Thomas Lipton and Sir Harry Lauder

Mr. and Mrs. Albert Victor du Pont

Will Rogers and family

Anita Loos and John Emerson

Mary Pickford and Douglas Fairbanks

Shipboard activities varied from the sublime to the preposterous. Swimming was one of the more popular and decorous sports, even when the pool was not adorned with bathing beauties like those posed aboard the *Rotterdam* (opposite); but taking a dip could be challenging, for a roll of the ship might translate at any moment into a pool-sized tidal wave. The ladies' pillow fight (below) was a bit of roughhouse staged on deck, with Mother Hubbards provided by the line. The torture chamber aboard the *Berengaria* (right center) was a variation on the Turkish steambath, a favorite antidote to over-indulgence. The tug-of-war (far right) gave third-class passengers aboard White Star's *Homeric* some free-form exercise.

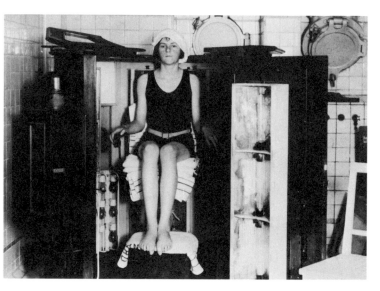

Every effort was made to bring all the comforts of a gentleman's club to shipboard: the *Laconia* offered a skeet shooting range (far left). If that was too fast, there were events like the turtle race (above), in which competitors jiggling long, taut strings urged cardboard terrapins across the deck. Golf came in several guises—from driving ranges to miniature courses like that on the *Ile de France* (opposite). Miniature golf was made to order for shipboard and gained its first favor there: funnels, scuppers, stanchions, and deck chairs, plus a few chalked-in obstacles, made for a lively game. Sometimes, it seemed, there was almost too much fun to bear. At left, two voyagers have found refuge in the *Britannic*'s smoking room.

Parents could enjoy brief reunions with their children (opposite, left) during the children's hour. For the rest of the day, ship's nannies were available. In good times, peace of mind of another sort could be found at the "stock exchange" (opposite, center), a chalkboard giving radio-received highlights of market activities. But the chief amusement on all vessels was food. Opposite right, a White Star bugler announces another sitting aboard the *Megantic*. A marble soda fountain provided snacks on the *Aquitania* (near right); tea or bouillon was served on the *Ile de France* (below); while genteel ambience made the *Leviathan*'s Winter Garden (far right) the perfect place to linger over an afternoon snack.

On the *Berengaria* (left), as elsewhere on the Atlantic, sunset was the signal to prepare for another glittering evening. As one brochure had it, the hour was one of "speculative detachment. . . . Only the soft wild rush of the wind is heard swirling against the impervious ship—and the faint stray cadence of a violin, a tinkling wisp of fugitive laughter." Thence, down to the cabin to dress for dinner. Black tie was in order in the *Ile de France*'s first-class dining room (opposite). After dinner, brandy and cigars materialized in the smoking room and a little later the orchestra began playing in the grand saloon, as below, on the *Statendam*. A publicity photograph (opposite, right) suggests that in the cocktail bar, the glamour was as heady as the drinks.

Nights to Remember

Prohibition, which started in 1919 and lasted into the early thirties, set the tone for night life. All but the American-owned ships kept well-stocked liquor lockers, and made the most of their competitive advantage. What repressed tippler could resist the blandishments of a French Line brochure that promised: "As you sail away, far beyond the range of amendments and thou-shalt-nots, those dear little iced things begin to appear, sparkling aloft on their slender crystal stems. . . . Utterly French, utterly harmless—and oh so gurglingly good!" But at least one traveler found the new giddy mood overdone: "The men begin as soon as they cross the three mile limit, and never cease until they are nearly insane."

In addition to legitimizing hard liquor, many European ships served wine gratis. Passengers on a typical eastbound trip on the *Ile de France* could avail themselves of 3,600 bottles of wine. Homeward bound, their drinking tended to be even more frenetic. At first U.S. officials ordered that all opened liquor bottles be dumped overboard before entering national waters. But the steamship companies preferred to give it away on the last night of the voyage—a courtesy that lasted until the government compromised and permitted the precious cargo to be locked away during the American turnaround.

In the evening, formal attire was de rigueur in first class. The rakish fellow greeting the dawn aboard the *Paris* (right) has obviously gone all out. But dressing up also took other, less predictable forms, as in the masquerade balls that were featured aboard most liners, including the *America* (left). On the day preceding such an event, the ship was likely to be bustling with purposeful passengers badgering the crew for bits of uniform, foul weather gear, and tools of the trade. Lest anyone be stymied for ideas, a small booklet, full of handy costuming tips, was available. Among its counsels was the advice that the boatswain might part with some rope from which to fashion a wig and that officers could supply bunting, whistles, white suits, and revolvers.

The Blue Ribbon Years

1929–1939

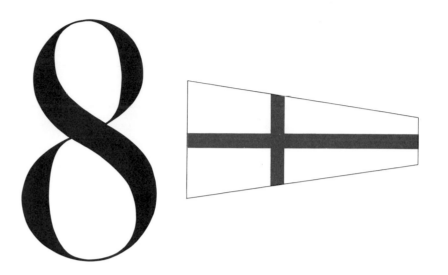

The contest for speed and luxury at sea is revived once more, as Germany's mighty *Bremen* races off to capture Blue Ribbon honors. . . . In the new decade, despite one of the worst economic slumps in shipping history, a new express liner appears almost every year and from almost every major shipping nation. . . . The speed record passes from one swift liner to another with astonishing regularity . . . until the appearance of the revolutionary *Normandie* and the staunch *Queen Mary*. . . . The fastest liners yet built, and the first to exceed 1,000 feet in length, they share the Blue Ribbon between them, leaving all other competitors in their wakes.

The *Normandie,* pictured in the dramatic French Line poster at right, was France's triumphant entrant into the "full steam ahead" competition for passengers that characterized the thirties. England's answer to the challenge was the *Queen Mary,* which set forth on her maiden voyage from Southampton in May, 1936, carrying the cheerfully overburdened passenger at left. As the rival lines knew only too well, passenger loyalty was not something any company could take for granted. The competitors were well aware that no matter how glorious a trip might have been, the temptation to try the newer, the faster, and the bigger under some other flag was always present. No line, no matter how successful, could afford to rest on its laurels.

NORMANDIE

Cⁱᵉ Gⁱᵉ TRANSATLANTIQUE

French Line

LE HAVRE — SOUTHAMPTON — NEW-YORK

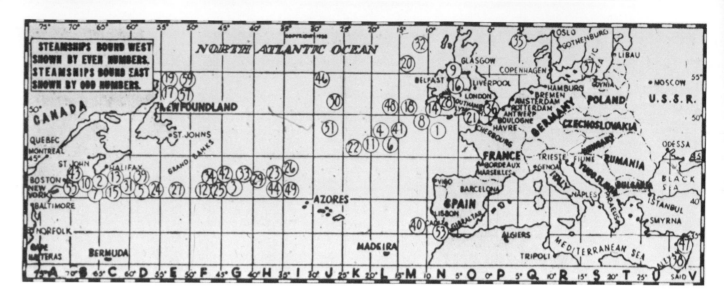

It was a mild evening in June, 1929, and the *Mauretania,* that graceful dowager of a ship, was steaming through the English Channel on yet another voyage between Southampton and New York. Twenty-two years had passed since her maiden crossing and still she was the fastest ship afloat; no liner yet had appeared to challenge her possession of the legendary Blue Ribbon speed record. But now, off in the twilight, the *Mauretania*'s crew and those few passengers who cared to bestir themselves could dimly perceive the lighted shadow of the ship that was about to end her long reign of supremacy.

The apparition glimpsed that evening was North German Lloyd's *Bremen,* returning at a leisurely pace from her acceptance trials on the Atlantic. Within a month she would recapture for Germany the Blue Ribbon honors that the *Mauretania* had taken from the *Kaiser Wilhelm II* two decades earlier. In so doing, she would return to Germany's merchant marine the preeminence it had enjoyed before the war.

The significance of the meeting did not escape the two captains, who signaled each other courteously before passing on. Their meeting signified the start of the last and greatest era of Blue Ribbon fever. Beginning with the *Bremen* in 1929, there were maiden crossings of new luxury express liners almost every year for a decade. And in that period the Blue Ribbon changed hands five times.

Paradoxically, this extraordinary era coincided with a worldwide economic depression, when cargo and passenger revenue was in decline. During the worst of it, liners were sailing half empty, a fifth of the world's shipping was standing idle, and thousands of men were out of work. But the slump made possession of the Blue Ribbon all the more urgent, since the prestige that went with the honor was worth a fortune in revenues to the company. There was still the question of finding money with which to build the giants—solved by the companies' pooling resources and obtaining government aid.

The first big merger came in 1931, when the long-time rivals Hamburg–America and North German Lloyd were combined. Under the new arrangement, the Lloyd's splendid sisters, *Bremen* and *Europa,* became the flagships of a new company, HAPAG–Lloyd.

Similarly, in 1932, Mussolini ordered the merger of three separate shipping lines into the Società per Azioni de Navigazione, or the Italian Line. That same year saw the maiden voyages of the speedy *Rex* and *Conte di Savoia*—originally intended as rivals but now teamed as running mates.

The merger of Cunard and the White Star Line followed, almost inevitably, in 1934. White Star, which had returned to British ownership in 1926, was having financial problems. For its part, Cunard had been forced to suspend building on the ship that was to have been Britain's answer to the *Bremen* and *Europa:* the ship that was as yet known only by its work order, "No. 534," but that would one day be christened *Queen Mary.*

At the John Brown Shipyards in Glasgow, the works sat idle for almost two and a half years until the government stepped in. Hoping to get men back to work and Britain back in the lead on the Atlantic, the government offered to provide the funds needed to complete the "No. 534" and to build a consort—on condition that Cunard and White Star agreed to merge. Agreement was swift. Work resumed and the *Queen Mary* was launched six months later.

Along with changes in the economic structure of the big companies, the thirties also brought a host of improvements in ship design and technology. The *Bremen,* the *Europa,* and later the French Line's *Normandie* gained crucial fractions of a knot of speed due to new streamlining techniques. These included replacing the usual sharp cutwater bow with a bulbous foot beneath the waterline, which cut

During a single day in July, 1938, fifty-three liners were on the Atlantic, as shown on the chart (opposite), a weekly feature of the New York *Herald Tribune*. Among them were the *Queen Mary* (11), *Normandie* (24), and *Ile de France* (29). In one of the innovations of the era, the *Ile de France* carried a seaplane on her afterdeck for delivering mail to the mainland up to seventy-two hours ahead of the ship's docking. In the photo below, the plane is seen strapped to its launching catapult on the ship's stern. After takeoff, the plane circles past the ship (bottom), heading for the airfield. HAPAG—Lloyd, hoping to catch the wave of the future, offered transatlantic passage via airship (right) in a breathless two and a half days.

down on drag by, in effect, filling in the vacuum that otherwise formed behind the bow wave.

In the drive for more efficient engines, Swedish–American introduced the first diesel-powered liner, the motorship *Gripsholm,* in 1925; and ten years later the *Normandie* became the first big Atlantic liner to run on turbo-electric power. The diesel, developed in Germany in the 1890s, ran at such high compression and temperature that fuel combustion was automatic. Turbo-electric power saved weight and space by using a turbine generator to drive an electric motor, which in turn was coupled to the propeller shaft.

The most significant developments of the age, however, were taking place not at sea but in the air. By the late 1930s, regular transatlantic passenger service was becoming a reality, with the *Graf Zeppelin* alone carrying some 28,000 passengers across the Atlantic during 437 round trips. HAPAG–Lloyd, in fact, served as agent for the airship; and for a time the *Ile de France* and the *Bremen* were launching airplanes from their decks in an effort to speed the mails to port ahead of the ship's arrival. But in trying to capitalize on the new developments, the shipping companies only hastened the day when airplanes would replace passenger liners altogether.

2½ DAYS TO EUROPE

DEUTSCHE ZEPPELIN-REEDEREI, G. m. b. H.
(German Zeppelin Transport Co.)
HAMBURG-AMERICAN LINE
NORTH GERMAN LLOYD
General Agents

Flagships of the New Regime

The Blue Ribbon sweepstakes of the 1930s got off to a smashing start with the maiden voyage of the *Bremen* in July, 1929 and with the announcement six months later that Italy was placing an order for a giant express liner, the *Rex.* The first event marked the recovery, in ten short years, of Germany's war-shattered shipping industry; the second heralded Italy's debut as a major shipping power.

The *Bremen* and her sister ship *Europa,* with their long, low lines and short, rakish funnels, had been launched with great fanfare on successive days in August, 1928. A year later, on her maiden voyage, the *Bremen* easily cut eight hours off the *Mauretania*'s best time, becoming the first ship to make the crossing in under five days. In 1930, she was joined in service by the even speedier *Europa.*

The first actual Blue Ribbon trophy, a silver cup put up by a British member of Parliament, was won by Italy's *Rex* for her record westbound crossing in 1933. She and her running mate, the *Conte di Savoia,* had been launched in the hope that they would lure American tourists to Italy. Outdoor swimming pools and broad sundecks added to the pleasures of crossing by the sunny southern route, in welcome contrast to the blanket-and-bouillon weather of a trip to northern Europe.

Her formidable hull afloat for the first time, the just-launched *Bremen* (opposite) is towed to a shipyard berth for fitting out. Eleven months later she was a seaborne powerhouse, ready to take the Atlantic speed record handily. The *Bremen*'s only competition, her sister ship *Europa,* was temporarily out of the running, having been swept by fire (left) shortly before completion and sunk by the weight of the water thrown onto the flames. She was refloated and ready to sail a year and $4.5 million later. Shown at top left and above, she looks as trim (and as oddly short-stacked) as her sister. A detail from the cover of a North German Lloyd brochure (shown on the opposite page) lists seven of the company's top liners of the thirties.

The bridge (above), the command center
of the quadruple-screw, steam turbine
powerhouse that drove the *Bremen* at
record speeds, was a quiet and relatively
uncrowded place, with most of the activity
centering around the wheel, chart table,
and ship's telegraph. In the public areas of
the *Bremen* and *Europa* (the two ships
were almost identical), the Germans made
some notable design changes. Rejecting
the fusty and elaborate decor found in
earlier liners, the designers favored the
sleek, understated style of Art Deco, creat-
ing such interiors as that of the swimming
pool (right) and the first-class dining
room (opposite, right). The *Europa*'s bar is
shown opposite above; while the drawing
on the cover of the *Bremen*'s "Farewell
Dinner" (opposite, left) suggests that
despite the ship's modern decor, Old World
charm was still to be found aboard the
German speed queen.

AUF WIEDERSEHEN!

★

ABSCHIEDS-ESSEN
FAREWELL-DINNER

Speed, Luxury, and Sunshine Too

In a scene that eerily prefigured her destruction at the hands of Allied bombers during World War II, Italy's Blue Ribbon winner *Rex* serves as a "target" for U.S. planes during a 1938 round of war games (opposite, top). The *Rex* and the *Conte di Savoia,* advertised in the brochure opposite, were the two prestige ships in the fleet of eleven Italian liners built between the wars. Italy's trump card in the transatlantic competition was the southern route that her fleet traveled. Starting in Genoa in the protected waters of the Mediterranean, the ships of the Italian Line could guarantee, theoretically, most of a voyage in brilliant sunshine and calm seas.

But in the rush to put the *Rex* and *Savoia* in service, mechanical shortcomings abounded. On her maiden voyage, the *Rex* was betrayed by her three turbo-generators and had to undergo an ignominious three days of repairs while anchored off Gibraltar. Still more serious was the inaugural mishap aboard the *Savoia*. Nine hundred miles off the coast of the United States, she blew a hole in her hull below the waterline and threatened to capsize before temporary repairs could be made.

Despite their inauspicious debuts, however, both ships managed to gain a considerable reputation for the kind of spaciousness exhibited in the *Savoia*'s main lounge (left) and "Hall" (above). The latter picture and those on the following pages were drawn to illustrate one of the Italian Line's publicity brochures.

"The Riviera itself comes out to meet you on the southern route," sang the advertisements of the Italian Line, as they displayed Lido-like scenes of the sort pictured here. The ladies' saloon (above) was notable for its large sliding glass walls, which opened onto the afterdeck. The sports deck (right) was dedicated to "lovers of the open air." Most remarkable of all the features aboard the *Rex* was the outdoor swimming pool (opposite), which was equipped with real sand and, when weather permitted, a cluster of beach umbrellas. Located on the topmost deck, between the ship's two funnels, the pool did in fact escape some of the winds the Atlantic usually delivered and on good days passengers could bask in temperatures that hovered around seventy degrees.

THE SWIMMING POOL

The Swimming pool, the Lido, the Veranda–Cafè, and the Bar make a magnificent en–semble which surpasses every expectation of the guests of the Special Class of the "REX".

Stormy Weather

The fair weather that made the southern route so appealing was a rarity on the northern Atlantic. During a midwinter passage, a stroll on deck could be a precarious business, with frozen spray coating the decks like boiler plate (as at left, on board the *Europa*). A ship's size was no defense against a rough crossing, as is evident in the photos opposite, left, taken on board the *Europa* (top) and *Aquitania* (center). The giant wave seen bearing down on the *Bremen* (opposite, right) struck so fiercely that the captain had to heave to in mid-Atlantic, and the ship was delayed three days on her voyage.

The gyrostabilizer (above) was a much heralded innovation on the *Savoia,* which was confidently called a "roll-less ship." But the gyros worked so well that the ship was *too* stable. Plowing through heavy seas on an absolutely even keel, she took a terrible beating. After a few such runs, use of the gyros was quietly abandoned.

All Dash and *Savoir Faire,* a Gallic Masterpiece Puts to Sea

The *Normandie,* bearing the name of the province from which all of France's finest steamers had set forth, was the Gallic challenge to Britain's *Queen Mary;* so long as they competed, the differences between them were largely a matter of style and gender. (Contrary to custom, the French refer to their ships as "he" not "she.")

The French nicknamed their contender "the floating debt," for the ship cost upward of $60 million. Subsidized from the start, the *Normandie* began service on May 29, 1935, a full year ahead of the *Mary,* though the St. Nazaire shipwrights had started work six months later than those at Clydeside.

In design and technology, the *Normandie* was the ship of the future, with turbo-electric propulsion and a rakishly streamlined hull. The ship's sides were nowhere parallel, while the clipper bow ended in the kind of bulbous forefoot that had been used so successfully on the *Bremen* and *Europa.* With these and other advantages, the *Normandie* dominated the Atlantic during 1935 and was, at 79,300 tons, the largest vessel afloat. When the even weightier *Mary* came along, the French promptly closed in some of the *Normandie's* deck space, thereby increasing the ship's gross tonnage and making "him" once again the largest of all ships.

The French were fond of comparing the *Normandie* to Versailles, and the allusion was apt. The ship's wine cellers (right, above) were as well-stocked, and the kitchen (right) as well-staffed as those in a royal palace. The first-class dining room (opposite, lower right) was an extraordinary 305 feet long. (Its uninterrupted length was made possible by the ship's divided uptakes, which rose on either side of the hull and came together just under the funnels.) The long sweep of the dining room's staircase, with its statue of *La Normandie* (opposite, top right), was the scene of some of the grandest entrances on the Atlantic. She also boasted the first real auditorium afloat, which the Paris Opera's corps de ballet inaugurated (center).

The Thirties' Promenade

Mr. and Mrs. Henry Ford

Helen Hayes and daughter Mary MacArthur

George Bernard Shaw

Marlene Dietrich

Ambassadors Anthony J. Drexel Biddle and Joseph P. Kennedy

The Douglas Fairbanks, Jrs. (Joan Crawford)

Greta Garbo

Pierre S. du Pont

Mr. and Mrs. Thomas Mann

Beatrice Lillie and Paul Hartman

Mr. and Mrs. Albert Einstein

The Windsors and friends

Laurence Olivier

King Ibn-Saud of Saudi Arabia

Gertrude Vanderbilt Whitney

Noël Coward

Ginger Rogers

King Ibn-Saud of Saudi Arabia

Maurice Chevalier

Amelia Earhart

Bernard Baruch

The *Queen Mary*'s engineers ran innumerable tank tests with scale models of various hull designs before settling on the tried and proven blade bow, which is seen in the dramatic photograph below, taken during the ship's fitting out. The scene opposite, photographed in May, 1936, shows the new liner at the end of her westbound maiden voyage being escorted to her pier on the west side of Manhattan by a flotilla of well-wishers. On this voyage, Cunard publicists provided free passage in first class to ninety prominent newsmen, so that no detail of the ship nor of the journey would be lost to the public; but when asked if the *Mary* was intended to snatch the Blue Ribbon trophy, Cunard's spokesmen feigned disinterest.

The Crowning Glory

From the drawing of the first blueprints to that celebrated day in May, 1936, when the *Queen Mary* nosed out of Southampton to begin her maiden run, every decision about the mammoth liner's design could be traced to her owners' quest for speed: the extra knots that would return Britain's merchant fleet to its former supremacy on the Atlantic.

That goal was almost the *Mary*'s undoing, for to gain even so small an advantage in speed it was necessary to build a ship of unprecedented size. A bigger power plant meant a larger hull, a larger hull meant greater length, greater length led to greater draft, and all this added up to a ship of 80,000 tons, far exceeding the 50,000-ton size that had been the superlative up to that time. New docks had to be built on both sides of the Atlantic; and the River Clyde, where the *Mary* was built, had to be dredged to a depth of forty feet. When Cunard was forced to stop work for lack of funds, the whole shipbuilding town of Clydebank was thrown into a depression. But the British government finally stepped in to save the project with a $3 million loan and a promise of $5 million more for a sister ship.

David Kirkwood, a Labor M.P. representing Clydebank, vividly described the feelings of national pride dashed and then reborn when Neville Chamberlain, then Chancellor of the Exchequer, announced the resumption of work: "For more than two years the Clyde had been like a tomb . . . a tomb with a vast and inescapable skeleton brooding over its silence. . . . It had sapped the vitality from a great town—aye, from a nation. . . . As [Chamberlain] spoke I saw . . . four thousand men moving along toward Brown's yard while the horn sang out the morning welcome. . . . And beyond the Clydebank I saw the glowing furnaces of Motherwell and Wishaw, the forges of Parkhead and the machine-shops and factories and wood-working yards of Glasgow. I saw the mines and the railways, the rolling-mills and rivet-factories full of energy and life. . . . I saw the makers of glass preparing 2500 square feet of glass for side windows and portholes . . . and weavers busy with carpet and linen; cabinet makers and upholsterers, joiners, carpenters, plumbers, electricians. . . . The silence of years broke into the music of work!"

Ultimately, the *Mary* did bring the coveted Blue Ribbon home to Great Britain, winning the prize on her sixth voyage with an officially recorded speed of thirty knots. During her long career, she was to enjoy a success and popularity that was unmatched by any other ship of her day.

"The Pride of the Clyde," as job No. 534 was known, towers over Clydebank (opposite, top), just as she dominated shipping news during the six years she was being built. Starting a new shift (opposite, center) are some of the four thousand shipwrights, fitters, engineers, electricians, and other workmen who made the mammoth undertaking a reality. In the near photograph, one of the liner's four thirty-five-ton manganese bronze propellers undergoes inspection.

The ship was launched on a nasty day in September, 1934, with full-dress ceremonies that brought out the entire royal family. Below, King George V and Queen Mary are seen at the microphones. To the right is Edward, Prince of Wales (the future Duke of Windsor). Sir Percy Bates, chairman of Cunard White Star, stands in attendance at far left. The honors were performed by the Queen, with golden scissors and a bottle of Australian wine.

Speed trials came after fitting out, almost two years later. Test runs, (right) were conducted with elaborate secrecy. Cunard even went so far as to code all communications between the bridge and the engine room, lest other ships in the vicinity intercept their radio signals. Later it was disclosed that the *Queen Mary* had reached an unofficial top speed of 35.42 knots. John Brown Shipyards proudly identified its major role in this grand maritime achievement by displaying a bronze plaque (below) aboard the ship.

BUILT AND ENGINED
BY
JOHN BROWN & COMPANY LIMITED
CLYDEBANK ENGINEERING & SHIPBUILDING WORKS
CLYDEBANK
AND OF
ATLAS WORKS SHEFFIELD

This cutaway view of the *Queen Mary*, with the various parts of the ship numbered and identified below, was painted at the time of her maiden voyage and published in the *Illustrated London News*. Misplaced during the war, it was recently rediscovered.

Sports Deck
1. Main mast.
2,3,4,5,6,7. Ventilators.
8. Staircase.
9. Space for deck sports, promenade, and deck tennis courts.
10,11. Tank room.
12. Directional aerials.
13. Semaphores.
14. Searchlights.
15. Chart room.
16. Wheelhouse and bridge.
17. Captain's and officers' quarters.

Sun Deck
18. Verandah grill.
19. Engineer officers' accommodation.
20. Engineers' wardroom.
21. Cinema projection room.
22. Gymnasium.
23. Squash racquets court.
24. Lift gear.
25. Wireless receiving room.
26. Staterooms and suites.
27. Forward staircase and lifts.
28. Staterooms and suites.

Promenade Deck
29. Cinema projection room.
30. Tourist smoking room.
31. Pantry.
32. Tourist entrance.
33. Smoking room.
34. Pantry.
35. After-end of long gallery (port side).
36. Staircase and lifts.

37. Ballroom.
38. Starboard gallery.
39. Pantry.
40. Stage of lounge.
41. Lounge.
42. Chair stowage.
43. Writing rooms.
44. Entrance.
45. Main hall and shopping center.
46. Drawing room.
47. Altar.
48. Children's playroom.
49. Forward staircase and lifts.
50. Cocktail bar and observation lounge.
51. Promenade.

Main Deck
52. Docking bridge.
53. Tourist lounge.
54. Tourist staircase and lifts.
55. Tourist writing room and library.
56. Staterooms and suites.
57. Staircase and lifts.

58. Storeroom.
59. Staterooms and suites.
60. Main staircase and lifts.
61. Furniture store.
62. Staterooms and suites.
63. Forward staircase and lifts.
64. Third-class garden lounge.
65. Cargo hatch.
66. Foremast.
67. Crow's nest (electrically heated).

"A" Deck
68. Cinema film store.
69. "A" deck tourist lounge.
70. Tourist entrance, staircase, and lifts.
71. Suites and bedroom accommodation.
72. Staircase and lifts.
73. Staterooms and suites.
74. Staircase and lifts.
75. Switch room.
76,77. Staterooms and suites.
78. Staircase and lifts.
79. Purser's office.

80. Staterooms and suites.
81. Forward staircase and lifts.
82. Third-class hairdresser's.
83. Third-class entrance.
84. Third-class smoking room.
85. Fore hatch.
86. Rope store.
87. Forecastle and anchor capstan.

"B" Deck
88. Crew.
89. Suites and bedroom accommodation.
90. Staircase and lifts.
91. Suites and bedroom accommodation.
92. Hairdresser's.
93. Staircase and lifts.
94. Suites and bedrooms.
95. Staircase and lifts.
96,97. Staterooms and suites.
98. Staircase and lifts.
99. Hairdresser's and beauty parlor.
100. Staterooms and suites.
101. Forward staircase and lifts.

102. Third-class Children's Playroom.	122. Private dining rooms.	142. Poultry, game, etc.	164. Specie room.	183. Shafts and shaft tunnels.
103. Third-class lounge.	123. Foyer.	143. Bacon and eggs.	165. Crew.	184. After engine rooms.
104. Mail-handling space.	124. Third-class dining saloon.	144. Grocery store.		185. Forward engine rooms.
105. Capstan gear.	125. Third-class entrance.	145. Hospital.	**"F" Deck**	186. Fan rooms.
106. Crew.	126. Third-class accommodation.	146. Dispensary.		187. No. 5 boiler room.
	127. Capstan gear and crew's space.	147. Printers' Shop	166. Tourist baggage room.	188. Air-conditioning plant.
"C" Deck		148. Third-class accommodation.	167. Bedroom accommodation.	189. After turbo-generator room.
	"D" Deck	149. Oil-filling station.	168. Tourist swimming pool.	190. Power station.
107. Crew.		150. Third-class accommodation.	169. Beer stores.	191. No. 4 boiler room.
108. Capstan space.	128. Crew.	151. Dressing rooms of swimming pool.	170. Lift well.	192. No. 3 boiler room.
109. Bedroom accommodation.	129. Suites and bedroom accommodation.	152. Swimming pool.	171. Wines and minerals.	193. Forward turbo-generator room.
110. Staircase and lifts.	130. Baggage lift well.	153. Kosher kitchen.	172. Garage.	194. Power station.
111. Suites and bedroom accommodation.	131. Suites and bedroom accommodation.	154. Third-class kitchens.	173. Registered mail.	195. No. 2 boiler room.
112. Staircase and lifts.	132. Tourist staircase and lifts.	155. Third-class accommodation.	174. Baggage.	196. No. 1 boiler room.
113. Tourist dining saloon.	133. Suites and bedroom accommodation.	156. Crew.	175,176. Mails.	197. Fan rooms.
114. Baker's shop.	134. Ales and stout.		177. Linen store.	198. Water-softening machinery.
115. Vegetable-preparing room.	135. Stores entrance.	**"E" Deck**	178. Baggage.	199. Tanks.
116. Kitchens.	136. Ice cream, butter, and milk.		179. Mail space.	200. Baggage.
117. Grill.	137. Fruit-ripening room.	157. Crew.		201. Mail space.
118. China pantry.	138. Fruit stores.	158,159,160,161. Suites and bedroom accom-	**Machinery and Hold**	202. General cargo.
119. Bar.	139. Vegetable and salad room.	modation.		203. Double bottom.
120. Private dining rooms.	140. Fresh and frozen fish.	162. Third-class accommodation.	180. Rudder.	
121. Restaurant.	141. Butcher's shop and meat store.	163. Mail discharge room.	181,182. Propeller, starboard side.	

Ocean Times

PUBLISHED ON BOARD CUNARD WHITE STAR LINERS

| Thursday, May 28, 1936 | R.M.S. QUEEN MARY | North Atlantic Edition |

The Commodore, Officers and Crew wish all passengers a happy and memorable voyage

HOW THE MAIDEN VOYAGE OF THE "QUEEN MARY" BEGAN

Quarter of a Million People at Southampton to See Her Off

Clear, sunny and dry weather favoured an afternoon of leading events, including the departure of the Cunard White Star liner Queen Mary on her maiden voyage across the Atlantic and the race for the Derby Stakes at Epsom—the broadcast of the events were followed with interest throughout Britain and round the world. Two seconds after the Derby winner passed the post the result had been transmitted to New York, Buenos Aires and Capetown. It was known in Melbourne within six seconds. (The Derby result appears in Page 6.)

Crowds estimated at 250,000 thronged Southampton Docks, the shores of Southampton Water and the heights of the Isle of Wight, and packed the decks of every available steamer and motor-boat, and aeroplanes flew overhead as the liner Queen Mary cast off and moved slowly from her berth at 3.30 p.m. G.M.T. Manœuvres were carried out perfectly, and in less than a quarter of an hour the great vessel gathered way and moved rapidly towards the sea. Many busy hours preceded the liner's departure, and every incident from the muster of the entire crew of 1,100 drill, with the launching of all the twenty-four unsinkable motor life-boats and the arrival of many distinguished passengers and their friends was watched with interest from the quayside.

In an interview the liner's Captain, Sir Edgar Britten, who received messages yesterday from all over the world, said he was sure the Queen Mary would ... English speaking

GREETINGS FROM THE EMPIRE

Sir Percy Bates' Broadcast of Thanks

The following message was broadcast from the Queen Mary early this morning by Sir Percy Bates, Bart., G.B.E., and included in the B.B.C. Empire News:

"As chairman of the company I feel deeply grateful that this great ship, of which we are all so proud, is now in the first stages of her maiden voyage to New York.

"I feel that the Queen Mary is not only a wonderful ship, but also a national achievement.

"I myself take pride in her because of my personal link with the men who made her what she is, the best piece of steelwork ever put together.

"I welcome the opportunity of giving my heartfelt thanks to all those throughout the British Empire who have sent messages of greeting and good will."

TOWNSEND PLAN INQUIRY

Contempt Recommendation by Committee

WASHINGTON.—The Townsend pension plan investigators recommended to the House of Representatives yesterday that Dr. Francis E. Townsend and two of his officers be cited for contempt and turned over to the United States attorney for trial. If convicted, Dr. Townsend and his two aides would face fines of $100 to $1,000 or up to one year in gaol, or both.

The committee acted after Mr. Sheridan Downey, Dr. Townsend's attorney, added his name to the list of those defying the committee by notifying it that he would not honour it by testifying.

The vote was six to one, many of the Townsend members of the committee posing it.

FOUR TIMES ROUND THIS DECK IS ONE MILE

The *Queen Mary*'s maiden voyage was run in an atmosphere bordering on euphoria, as is evident by the front page stories appearing in the *Ocean Times,* Cunard's shipboard daily (opposite, left). With national pride so thoroughly tied up in the *Mary*'s success, no detail of ship management was considered beneath concern, and the crew was held to military standards of performance. Fingernail inspection (opposite, center) was part of the stewards' typical eighteen-hour workday. The passengers' day, by contrast, ran the gamut from languorous to leisurely, with topside hikes among the most strenuous of activities; the plaques on the promenade deck (opposite, below) announced that four times around is equivalent to a mile and that the speed record to beat was Lord Burghley's once-around in full evening dress in fifty-eight seconds.

The *Mary*'s lavishly decorated public rooms included the observation lounge with its Art Deco bar (left), and the main dining room (above), which seated eight hundred and was decorated with a mural of the North Atlantic.

Gracious Consorts of the Blue Ribbon Fleet

Without the fanfare that attended the 1000-foot giants, the thirties also brought some fine ships in the 700-foot class. The new *Mauretania* (left), which bore the proud name of the earlier Cunard favorite, made just two crossings before World War II broke out. Two handsome Holland–America ships, shown above, were the *Statendam* (foreground) and the *Nieuw Amsterdam*. The latter carried 1,187 passengers and cost a mere $12 million to build—a fine example of what could be done with a budget less than one-fifth the size of the *Normandie*'s. The Canadian Pacific's *Empress of Britain* was remarkable both for her speed and her versatility: summers she captured Canadian and midwestern American trade by running to Quebec, (opposite, left); winters she was a cruise liner in southern waters. The *America* (opposite), was launched August 31, 1939. President Roosevelt acclaimed the launch "one of the most important events to take place in the world this year." The next day German troops marched into Poland, indirectly putting an end to the *America*'s peacetime career and changing the future of every passenger ship afloat.

In the Line of Duty

1939–1945

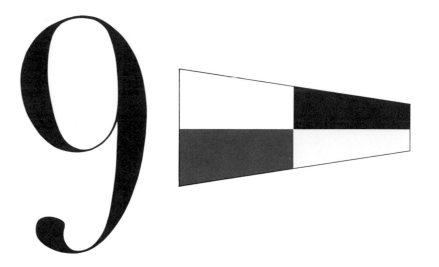

Stalked again by the dogs of war, the Atlantic liners race for cover . . . and the newly completed *Queen Elizabeth* makes her maiden voyage in secret. . . . Bombs, torpedoes, and saboteurs take their toll on Allied and Axis shipping alike, destroying some of the finest liners of the prewar era . . . while the beautiful *Normandie* meets a bitter end at the hands of careless workmen. . . . Meantime, one by one, the Allied liners come out of hiding. Painted battleship gray, with their grand saloons converted to mess halls and their cabins to barracks and wardrooms, they take up the task of ferrying troops and supplies to the war zones of Europe and the Pacific.

Garbed in wartime gray, the Dutch liner *Nieuw Amsterdam* hurries across the sea with her precious cargo of troops. During her war service on the Atlantic and Indian oceans she carried more than 350,000 men.

On sea as on land, the first days of World War II had a dreadful familiarity to people who remembered the start of the Great War twenty-five years before. Again, there was the rush of ships toward safe harbors. Again, there were thousands of travelers stranded as sailings were canceled and liners put in abruptly at unexpected ports.

This time, however, any uncertainties about Germany's intentions were laid to rest right at the start. On September 3, 1939, just hours before Britain declared war, the British liner *Athenia,* en route to Montreal with 1,418 persons on board, was torpedoed and sunk by a U-boat off the northern coast of Ireland. One hundred and twelve people lost their lives. Notice was thus brutally served: there would be no niceties shown toward civilians in this new and terrible war; British and Allied liners were to be sunk without warning.

When the war started, many liners that might have become prime targets for attack were already well beyond the reach of submarines and other dangers. Victims of age, accident, and the Depression, they had one by one joined the parade to the ship-breakers. The *Mauretania,* the queen mother of the turbine era, had been broken up in 1935, as had the *Olympic.* The *Berengaria,* once Germany's proud *Imperator,*

was scrapped by Cunard White Star in 1938. America's *Leviathan* (ex-*Vaterland*) was also broken up in 1938; while the third of the one-time German giants, the *Majestic* (ex-*Bismarck*), caught fire and sank in September, 1939, while being fitted out as a training ship in Scotland. France's elegant *Paris,* also a victim of fire, lay in the ooze beside her pier at Le Havre, where she remained throughout the war.

The biggest of the new liners, the *Queen Mary* and the *Normandie,* were tied up side by side in New York when the war began. So was the *Ile de France.* For months, the three lay idle while the tides piled sand up under their keels and governments pondered their fates. Then, in March, 1940, they were joined by a mysterious newcomer, a great gray giant of a ship, the *Queen Elizabeth.* Unfinished and almost empty, she had slipped away from her fitting-out pier on the Clyde, where she had been a sitting duck for German bombers, and had completed her maiden crossing in secret. In the months ahead, she and her sister *Mary* were to play an important part in helping to defeat the Axis powers, sailing over a million miles and carrying some two million service men.

The war brought an end to the Blue Ribbon liners of Germany and Italy. The only one to survive

was the *Europa;* and her dash for cover at the start of the conflict was no less indecorous than the *Elizabeth*'s. On August 24, 1939, she was mid-Atlantic when word came of the German–Russian nonaggression pact. Her lights were promptly dimmed, her portholes covered, and her stops at Southampton and Cherbourg were canceled—to the alarm of her British and American passengers. She reached Bremerhaven safely but never again sailed as a German ship. Once bombed by the British, then scheduled for destruction by the German high command, she survived the one and avoided the other, only to fall into American hands in May, 1945. Her conversion into the French *Liberté* began a year later.

The *Bremen,* all but empty, slipped out of New York on her last ocean crossing on the evening of August 30, 1939, just hours before Hitler's armies invaded Poland. With her band blaring "Deutschland Uber Alles," she steamed down the Narrows, destination unknown. Eight days later she turned up in Russia's Arctic port of Murmansk, painted gray and prepared for scuttling in case she had been captured by British warships. She lay low for a few months, then sped down the Norwegian coast to Bremerhaven. There, she was destroyed by fire in 1941, possibly the victim of sabotage.

By the late 1930s, the swastika flags, flying from the taffrail of Germany's speed queens, *Bremen* and *Europa* (right), were already lending an ominous tone to the publicists' typically romantic vision of life aboard an ocean liner. In the photo opposite, taken August 29, 1939, a passenger aboard the *Aquitania* peers warily from beneath a window that has been blacked out in anticipation of war. The ship was to have been scrapped in the thirties but was saved for war service, during which she carried some 339,000 troops and refugees. The *Mauretania* was not so lucky. In 1935, just four years short of the war, she was brought to Rosyth, Scotland, where she was piped out of service (below) and then broken up.

Italy's *Rex* and *Conte di Savoia* remained in service through May, 1940, leading many to believe that Mussolini would keep Italy out of the war. But by mid-June the bubble had burst. All voyages were canceled. The Italian Line announced that sailings would resume "early in September, when the war is over." Instead, the *Savoia* was hidden among the marshes near Venice, where she was bombed and sunk in September, 1943. A year later, near Trieste, the *Rex* too was sunk.

The havoc of war was not visited upon the Fascist fleet alone. Of the largest Allied liners, the *Normandie* met an inglorious end when she accidentally caught fire at her New York pier. Canada's luxurious *Empress of Britain,* the largest ship of any type to be lost during the war, was bombed and sunk off the coast of Ireland in 1940. (Fitted out as a transport capable of carrying 8,000 troops, she was fortunately carrying only 643 persons at the time. But 45 people died.)

Britain's air supremacy over the eastern Atlantic, however, prevented any other major vessels from being destroyed. Although 574 British and North American merchantmen were lost on the North Atlantic, more than 75,000 crossings of all kinds were safely made during the war years.

A quintet of some of the finest liners ever built lay side by side in New York Harbor in the early months of 1940 (left). They are (from top): Italy's *Rex,* still in service on the southern route; the *Aquitania;* the *Queen Mary,* being repainted for war service; the *Normandie;* and the *Ile de France.* Dutch liners not caught in the heavy German bombing of Rotterdam in May, 1940, hurried to neutral ports and were made ready for war (as seen in the photograph at right). Gun mounts are also visible on the afterdeck of the *Aquitania* (opposite) as she scurries for England in September, 1939. Soon she was on her way to Sydney, Australia, where she was to be fitted out as an Allied troop transport. The last survivor of that proud array of liners built with four stacks (there had been fourteen such ships altogether), the *Aquitania* was the only liner to serve in both World Wars. Known alternately as the "Grand Old Lady" or "Old Irrepressible," she traveled half a million miles on Allied missions during the Second World War.

Battleship gray, the *Queen Elizabeth* slips into New York Harbor (above) ending her perilous maiden voyage. Ship cognoscenti immediately noticed the copper cable fastened around her hull (left, arrows). Electrical current was sent through this "degaussing strip" to neutralize Germany's magnetic Gauss mines. In the photo above right, the *Ile de France* ferries bombers and twelve thousand tons of war matériel to France in the last desperate weeks before that country's fall to Germany. The British seized control of the ship in Singapore after fights between Gaullist and Vichy crewmen. Converted during four months of intensive work in New York, the *Ile* went to work as a British trooper in 1941.

In 1940, the new *Mauretania* (right) was already armed when she steamed out of New York Harbor in a downpour, bound for Australia and duty as a troopship. Meanwhile, the war forced the United States Line's new ship *America* to start life as a cruise ship (flyer, opposite left). However, she and the *Manhattan,* were soon rescuing Americans stranded in Europe. Opposite, the *Manhattan,* boldly proclaiming her neutrality should she chance on a U-boat, heads out to sea. After the United States entered the conflict, the *America, Manhattan,* and *Washington* were the largest ships in the Navy's drafted fleet. Renamed *West Point, Wakefield,* and *Mount Vernon* respectively, they ferried troops to war zones around the world.

Brilliant Vacation Voyages in American Waters by the luxurious New

AMERICAN FLAG LINER

AMERICA

largest, finest liner ever built in the United States

TO THE AMERICAN AND NEUTRAL ISLANDS OF

ST. THOMAS
(VIRGIN ISLANDS)

SAN JUAN
(PUERTO RICO)

PORT AU PRINCE
(REPUBLIC OF HAITI)

HAVANA
(CUBA)

★

12 Days $150 up

★

Maiden Voyage
AUGUST 10
1940

NO PASSPORTS OR VISAES REQUIRED

UNITED STATES LINES

In a view from an RAF bomber (left), rockets zero in on Italy's *Rex* off Capo d'Istria, near Trieste. More than a hundred rockets found their mark, and the ship was sunk. Above, off the coast of Florida, crewmen escape in a lifeboat from the German ship *Columbus* (background), after having burned and scuttled her to prevent her capture by a British destroyer. The German bombing of Britain's *Lancastria* (top), in which 3,000 troops died, was the worst Allied naval disaster. "Two bombs struck us," a survivor wrote. "The bottom was blown clear out. . . . The bullets tore up the planking around my feet. By this time . . . the list was at least 40° . . . I scrambled up the high side and *walked down the ship's side.*"

The *Normandie*'s Blazing End

The conversion of the *Normandie* into the troopship *Lafayette* (above) began soon after the United States entered the war and seized all French ships berthed in America. Seven weeks later, as the ship's transformation was nearing completion, the *Normandie* became the hearth for a holocaust (right). The blaze was started by careless workmen, when an acetylene torch came too close to a pile of flammable life jackets and mattresses. But it was more than the workmen's carelessness. The War Department and Navy Department had been taking turns changing specifications, while at the same time demanding that the enormous task be completed in a few weeks. Supervision was inadequate, and there were few fire precautions.

Like some great beached sea creature, the *Normandie* lies in the ice (left) after capsizing under the weight of the water poured into her by firemen. In the stern view (top left), her useless screws protrude at a grotesque angle, and her gangway lies draped along her giant flank. Her once grand staircase, now charred and water-logged, was photographed (above) before she rolled over.

The loss of the ship was partly the result of monumental confusion. No one who knew the ship was allowed to take charge of the fire-fighting operation. The vessel was inundated with thousands of gallons of fatal top weight and so capsized.

The resurrection of the mired monster (opposite, top) took twenty months and was a triumph of salvage engineering. Public-spirited citizens offered numerous

suggestions for setting the ship afloat, including air bags, ping-pong balls, ice cubes, dynamite, and divine intercession. The Navy chose more traditional methods. Salvagers cut off the ship's superstructure and removed tons of debris. Then they remade the bulkheads watertight. The submerged half of the hull was patched together by a team of four hundred divers, who had to do their work while groping through the slime, slick, and sewage of New York Harbor. A yardstick (seen in the photo) measured each painfully recaptured inch during the grand finale—six weeks of pumping.

Once raised, however, authorities found the *Normandie* not worth repairing. The great ship, now no more than a battered hull, was dragged off ignominiously to the junkyard (opposite, below).

Troopers Once Again

An extraordinary parade of ships steamed out of Suez on January 25, 1943: the *Queen Mary, Ile de France, Aquitania, Nieuw Amsterdam,* and the *Queen of Bermuda.* Far from their usual tracks on the Great Circle Route, the five liners were now serving as troop transports. Their mission was to return Australia's entire Middle East expeditionary force of thirty-one thousand men to defend their homeland and help in the offensive against Japan.

Spectacular as the convoy may have been, it was just one of the many wartime missions for the Allied fleet of hundreds of converted liners and freighters. In the years before giant air transports did the job, ships provided the lifeline of the Allied war effort, carrying the men and supplies needed on the European and South Pacific fronts. Tremendous numbers were carried on British and American merchant ships; American troops alone totaled some four and a half million men.

That these millions could be transported swiftly and safely was a tribute to big liners like the *Queen Mary* and the *Queen Elizabeth,* which, on some voyages, carried as many as sixteen thousand men. Too fast for other ships to keep up with, they rarely traveled in convoy. Their speed was their best defense against the enemy, and convoys only slowed them down.

Troops line the rails of the *Mauretania* (opposite, below), one of the flotilla of steamships that sailed to and from the war zones. Out at sea, America's *Wakefield* (left), formerly the *Manhattan,* steams along in convoy, while a hovering blimp watches for submarines. On southern ocean convoys, like the one opposite (top), shorts and shirt sleeves were favored by officers and men. The big three-stacker in the distance is the *Queen Mary,* making a rare convoy appearance. She and the *Queen Elizabeth* were often on southern seas, ferrying Australian troops and supplies. In the photo above, the sisters are seen passing each other off the headlands of Sydney, Australia.

The two-hour zigzag course delineated at right was used by the *Queen Mary* and other ships as a defense against submarines. It was while she was zigzagging off the coast of Scotland in October, 1942, with ten thousand American troops on board, that the *Mary* suffered her only major wartime accident. The British escort cruiser *Curacoa,* which had come out to meet her, inadvertently cut across her bow and was sliced in two. The cruiser sank in minutes, and 329 of her 430-man crew were killed. Ordered never to endanger his own ship and passengers by stopping to rescue survivors, the *Mary*'s captain kept up speed and made it into port—despite a fearfully crumpled bow (far right).

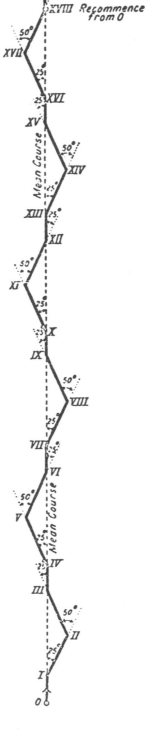

The surroundings were familiar, but life aboard the converted liners was very different than it had been in peacetime. A first-class cabin on the *Queen Mary* served as barracks for twelve, with just enough room for U.S. Army Air Force personnel (above) to sleep, to shoot craps, or—as the official caption would have it—to "gather around a map to detail their exploits in the European theatre." The mural in the *Queen Mary*'s first-class restaurant (near right) may have looked the same as ever, but the atmosphere was distinctly mess hall when two thousand men were fed at one sitting. The shuffleboard court (right, top) was a remnant of more carefree days; while a nursery on the *Queen Mary* (right, bottom) was used as an RAF orderly room.

In a scene reminiscent of the emigrant
ships (below, left) troops take the air
aboard the jam-packed *Wakefield*. To keep
the men fit and to prevent the malaise born
of boredom, physical training classes were
held aboard troopships (below). The
enormously complicated task of transport-
ing huge numbers of fighting men across
the oceans was accomplished with
amazingly little hardship to the troops
themselves. One British writer commented
that the liners were managed with "a
sensitive understanding of the limits of
human tolerance. . . . As a result," he
continued, "these free men, in grand total
of hundreds of thousands, were brought
through their hard experience physically
whole, sane, and well fed."

With thousands of men being carried on a single ship, every precaution was taken to insure their safety. In hostile waters, the men were ordered on deck in their Mae Wests (as above, on the *Queen Mary*) to reduce casualties in case of an attack. Allied governments did their best to conceal sailing dates and destinations even from the GIs involved. Posters like the one at right were part of an ongoing campaign warning those who stayed behind not to reveal anything they knew about troop sailings. When transports traveled as hospital ships (opposite), they could not claim Red Cross neutrality despite the helplessness of their passengers. In these photographs, orderlies feed wounded Americans aboard the *Queen Elizabeth;* and a young warrior, bound in a chest-high cast, heads for home on the *Wakefield*. Morale was generally high on the troopships, but there was always the fear of being spotted by a stalking U-boat or fighter plane.

A careless word...

...A NEEDLESS SINKING

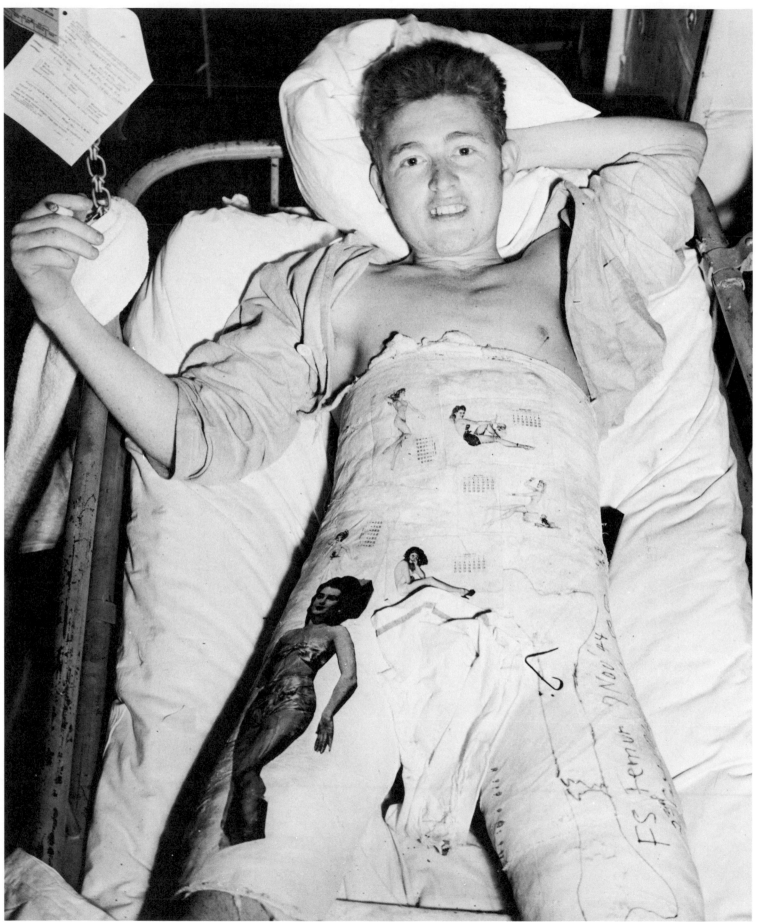

In 1945, with their wartime duties and dangers past, the liners had the job of taking millions of American, Canadian, and other Commonwealth troops home. At left, the aging *Aquitania,* performing one last service for the Allies, arrives in New York with eight thousand troops aboard; while above, the *Queen Elizabeth,* packed with humanity, rushes eager servicemen back to the United States. In February, 1946, the *Queen Mary* was relieved of her troop transport duties and was given a new assignment: that of ferrying thousands of GI brides to their new homes in America— and as many as nine hundred fifty babies per westbound crossing. A few of these new Americans are seen strolling along the *Mary*'s deck in the photograph at right.

The Last Voyages

1945–1977

With the troops home and the seaways safe once more, Europe and the Atlantic liners play host to a new army: platoons of vacationing tourists. . . . Britain's *Queen Mary* and *Queen Elizabeth*, working in tandem at last, lead the postwar cavalcade of liners . . . until the S.S. *United States*, sleek as a yacht and fast as an express train, sweeps the Blue Ribbon honors. . . . But speed soon counts little on the North Atlantic. . . . With jet aircraft making even the fastest liners obsolete, fewer people choose to make the crossing by sea . . . and one liner after another abandons the Great Circle Route for good and for all.

Leaving passengers' friends and relatives on the pier, the *America,* flagship of the United States Lines in the years just after World War II, prepares to slip out of her berth along New York's Steamship Row.

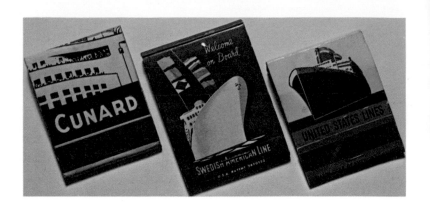

For the *Queen Mary* it was the sound of carpenters' tools that marked the end of World War II: the sound of workmen planing or replacing the wooden rails on which countless servicemen had carved their names and initials. For the *Queen Elizabeth,* the end was signaled by the blast of her horn as she sailed out of Southampton on her official maiden voyage in October, 1946—eight years after her launching. And for Germany's *Europa,* the war's end brought the sound of strange voices: workmen chattering among themselves in French as they painted her bow and stern with a new name and a new home port: *Liberté,* Le Havre.

For these and the other liners that were lucky enough to have survived the hostilities, the postwar years were full of promise. Hardly had the last gun been stilled when thousands of American tourists, guidebooks in hand, began to descend upon Europe.

The tourist business was a tremendous boon to the shipping companies, especially to the British ones, and most especially to Cunard. In a single month— July, 1950—British liners carried 145,000 Americans to Europe, and the number was growing every year. Cunard, with its two *Queen*s now carrying out the weekly service for which they had been intended more than twenty years before, was

enjoying the most profitable period in its history—the *Queen*s alone earning $50 million a year.

It did not require any particularly keen business sense to realize that tourism was the wave of the future. Just as the steamship companies had responded to the turn-of-the-century emigrant flood by building more and bigger ships, the companies now began competing for their share of the summer emigrant traffic by converting more and more passenger space to "tourist class."

The trend started in 1952, with Holland– America's small *Maasdam* and *Ryndam,* in which the eight hundred tourist-class passengers were given the run of the ship, while the forty or so first-class travelers were confined to a small space on the upper deck. Other lines began following suit, with one company after another eliminating second- third-, and cabin-class accommodations in favor of a "class-less" tourist class.

Meantime, encouraged by the rising demand for inexpensive but comfortable passage across the Atlantic, every major steamship company had begun building a new fleet of liners. Mostly the new ships were designed to serve a dual function: as transatlantic liners and as long-distance cruise ships. The majority were medium sized, like Cunard's *Caronia,* Swedish–

American's *Gripsholm,* and the Italian Line's elegant sister ships, *Andrea Doria* and *Cristoforo Colombo.* The one big liner launched in the fifties was the *United States,* whose record-breaking maiden voyage in July 1952, made it seem, for a time at least, as if the North Atlantic were on the brink of a spectacular new era of Blue Ribbon competition.

Within a few years, however, the transatlantic speed record became irrelevant. True, the volume of traffic across the Atlantic continued to increase. In 1956, more than a million people made the ocean crossing—the first time that many people crossed in more than twenty years. But as fast as steamship travel was growing, airline travel was growing faster.

Aircraft technology had been fairly primitive in the prewar years, and had posed no threat to steamships. But by the 1950s, airplanes had advanced to the point where it was possible to cross the Atlantic in twelve to fourteen hours. In the cramped quarters of a Constellation, the flight was still something of an endurance test. But the introduction of passenger jets in the late fifties reduced the crossing time to six and a half hours nonstop.

Flying meant that during their limited time abroad, the harried businessman and the tourist with a short vacation saw less of the sea and more of the sights.

On September 3, 1957, during the peak of the postwar tourist boom, a dozen liners pulled into New York Harbor, making it the biggest single day in the port's history. A total of 9,300 passengers debarked, causing horrendous traffic jams. Shown in the group photo are seven of the liners that tied up in Manhattan that day: from left, the motorship *Britannic,* the *Queen Mary,* the *Mauretania,* the French Line's *Flandre,* the Greek *Olympia,* the *United States,* and the *Independence.* As mementos of their crossings, few tourists could resist making off with some souvenir. Among the most easily pocketed were silverware, napkins and, of course, matchbooks and ashtrays, a selection of which is shown on these pages.

And that suited more and more travelers just fine. In the landmark year of 1957, as many people crossed the Atlantic by air as crossed it by sea. Soon the decline in steamship business became precipitous.

The contest between the liner and the airplane was not an equal one. In the past, the greatest challenge the steamships had to face—aside from the Atlantic itself—had been the competition between steamship lines. Throughout all the improvements in design and technology that had kept one steamship company ahead of its competitors, the primary goal had always been the same: to get people across the ocean as quickly and safely as possible, with as much comfort as passengers could afford and the Atlantic would allow. Now airplanes were performing that function so much more effectively that they were destroying the Atlantic liner's chief reason for being.

Unable to compete on their old terms, the steamship companies began praising the virtues of an unhurried crossing. "Getting there is half the fun," Cunard proclaimed. And even a voyage on the *United States,* the fastest liner ever built, was being billed as "a five day adventure in the lost art of leisure." Still the passenger trade dwindled; liners were taken off the North Atlantic run every year.

Queens of the Postwar Fleet

Dominating the postwar era on the North Atlantic were the *Queen Mary* and *Queen Elizabeth*. The *Mary* was restored to her old luxurious self (below) in 1947, while the *Elizabeth* (below, left) was only making her debut in polite society. Dominating the postwar passenger lists, meanwhile, were the Americans: students, vacationers, and dauntless school teachers —like those seen opposite coping with the rigors of Pier 90. For them, a sailing was an exciting novelty. But to the men on the bridge it was all business. In the photo of the *Elizabeth*'s flying bridge (opposite, below), five men conduct a departure. They are, from left: the undocking pilot, the second mate, the harbor pilot, the captain, and the second officer.

Aboard the liners that survived the war, peaceful moments like the one shown opposite, right, were a welcome relief from the anxieties of wartime crossings. Ranking among the most popular ships of the postwar era was the *Ile de France* (below). Requisitioned by the French government to carry troops to Indochina, she was afterwards completely reconditioned, stripped of one of her three funnels, and returned to transatlantic service in 1949. A year later, she was joined by the French Line's *Liberté* (ex-*Europa*), shown here in New York Harbor (opposite, left). Holland–America's flagship, the *Nieuw Amsterdam,* at left, seen from the deck of the *United States,* resumed her New York schedule in 1947.

Air travel might have the edge on speed, but postwar liners still held the monopoly on pleasant memories, as suggested in these photos taken aboard the two *Queen*s. "Boots" (left) was the proud professional who kept a high glow on his charges' shoes. Lifeboat drill was a serio-comic event designed to familiarize passengers with the mysteries of the boat, a Mae West, and a square knot. Culinary reputations now depended more on show than on the imaginativeness of the menu. During the gala dinner (right), passengers endured the ritual of wearing funny hats. Pastry cooks (center, right) and waiters with a flourish for flambé (bottom, right) tended to rank higher in most passengers' favor than the *sauciers*.

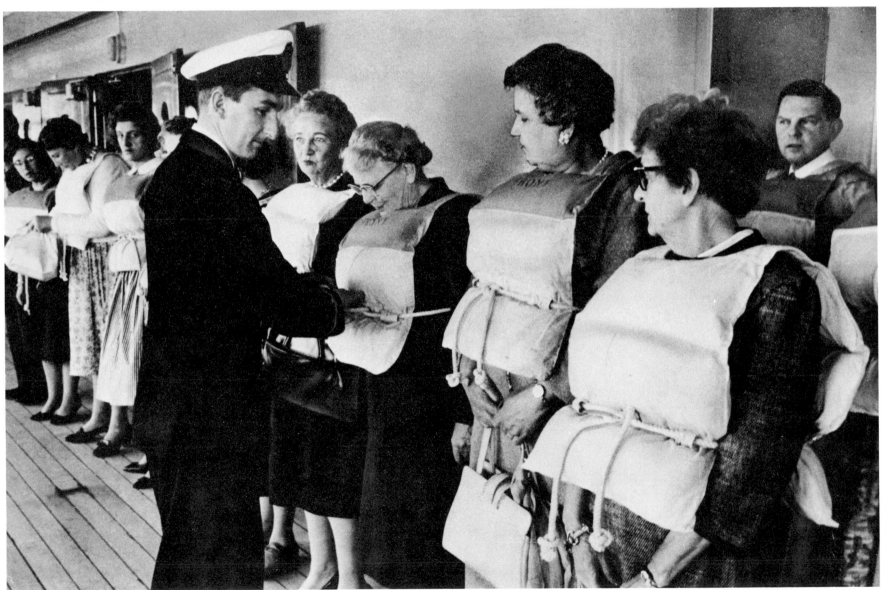

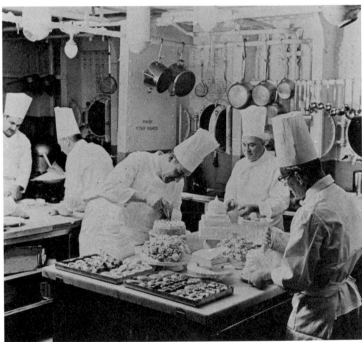

The number of miles traveled each day at
sea had for years been the basis of an
elaborate auction pool, played for high
stakes in the first-class smoking room
(below). Pool numbers were drawn by lot
and passengers either kept their draw or
bid for mileage figures more to their fancy.
Everyone on board could play the more
informal "hat pool," bidding from $2 to
$10 on mileage numbers. The bidding
closed at noon, the correct number was sent
down from the bridge, and the day's
winnings were awarded. After lunch
itineraries were planned and letters were
written in the library (below, right). The
voyage ended on the pier under the
gaze of the customs officers. At right is the
first-class customs area in Southampton.

America's Blue Ribbon Triumph

Commodore Harry Manning, captain of the S.S. *United States,* was perhaps being too ingenuous when he described his ship's record-breaking maiden voyage of July 4–7, 1952: "I was not particularly trying for any record," he said, "this ship just goes at that speed."

"That speed" was an average of 35½ knots, or about 41 land miles an hour—faster than any ship had yet traveled or was likely to travel again. The *United States* slashed the *Queen Mary*'s best time by an astonishing ten hours, covering the official course—from Ambrose Lightship outside New York to Bishop Rock Light House off the tip of Cornwall— in just three days, ten hours, and forty minutes. Many of her two thousand passengers stayed up all night to see the ship speed past its eastern mark, and even Commodore Manning had to confess that "my hands trembled with excitement as we passed Bishop Rock." The record crossing brought the Blue Ribbon to America for the first time since the heyday of the Collins Line in the 1850s.

No steamship company would ever admit publicly that it was trying for the Blue Ribbon. That might have brought bad luck, and would certainly have jeopardized the company's prestige if the attempt failed. But however cautious the company and Com-

modore Manning may have been about saying so, the Blue Ribbon was one of the reasons the *United States* had been built. The hope was that the glamour of a Blue Ribbon winner would capture for America's entire merchant fleet a healthy share of the trans-atlantic tourist trade. Although she cost some $77 million to build, the new ship stood to earn some $25 million in revenue every year.

Unlike previous Blue Ribbon winners, however, the *United States* was not intended primarily for commercial passenger service. First and foremost, she was designed for quick conversion to a troop transport in the event of a national emergency, and she was capable of carrying fourteen thousand troops.

Two-thirds the tonnage of either of the *Queen*s, though just as spacious, she was narrow enough to slip through the Panama Canal; and she could steam across the Pacific and back without refueling or taking new stores aboard. The extensive use of aluminum in her hull, superstructure, and interiors—only the piano and the butcher's block were of wood—may have made her seem rather austere; but it also made her as fireproof as a ship could be. That the *United States* transcended her military origins to become an immensely popular Atlantic liner was a high tribute to her architects and builders.

As sleek and functional as a space rocket, the *United States* (right) looks every inch the machine for transportation that she was built to be. "Well, why not?" said William Gibbs, her designer. "The *United States* is a ship, not an ancient inn with oaken beams and plaster walls." Below, she undergoes trials off the Virginia coast under top security conditions intended to keep her speed a military secret. Not for fourteen years was it known that she could reach a top speed of 42 knots (48 mph). Posters, which usually exaggerate, were right on target with the banner headlines (left). As one Britisher quipped: "After the loud and fantastic claims . . . it comes as something of a disappointment to find them all true."

A pith-helmeted Gibbs confers over blue-prints with several associates (opposite, top) at the Newport News, Virginia, ship-yard. For Gibbs, the two years of building and outfitting were the culmination of more than thirty-five years of experience, beginning with his conversion of the *Vaterland* into the *Leviathan* in the World War I period and his work on scores of military-class ships thereafter. In the aerial view of the yards (opposite, left), the hull of the *United States* begins to take shape in dry dock, its massive hull dwarfing another Gibbs ship, the eleven-year-old *America,* which was laid up in the adjacent dry dock for repairs.

One of the new ship's two fifty-foot funnels is shown (opposite, center) as it awaits installation. The streamlined fins that capped it were designed to carry the smoke and soot away from the afterdeck. The funnels were made of lightweight aluminum, as was the rest of the super-structure, an innovation that was designed to lower the center of gravity and make the ship more stable.

Eventually, the *United States,* seventy percent completed, was floated free of her dry dock and towed to a nearby slip where she is shown (at left) being made ready for her trial runs. Among the last tasks was the moving in of "fifties-modern" aluminum chairs, a few of which are seen in the photo at right. Gibbs' concern with achieving maximum stability ex-tended even to considering the weight of the furniture, which was reportedly figured down to the last twenty-five pounds.

Photos like those of the control panels (above) and the water pipes (right) were classified until 1968, when the secrecy surrounding the *United States* was finally lifted. It was then revealed that her four turbines were capable of producing not the 150,000 horsepower originally claimed but 240,000 h.p. But extravagance ended there, and public rooms like the dining saloon (far right) were done in an uncluttered modern style. Gibbs's concern with fireproofing led to a ban on oil-paint murals, but metal sculptures (as seen in the photo at far right) decorated the ship.

A popular vessel, the *United States,* seen opposite sailing past midtown Manhattan, had a long career. But through most of her seventeen years she suffered badly from competition with the airlines. Withdrawn from service in 1969, she was bought by the United States government and is presently tied up in the James River awaiting sale.

Andrea Doria

"ITALIAN LINE"

Collision off Nantucket Light

With the *Rex* and the *Conte di Savoia* destroyed by Allied bombers, the Italian Line brought out a new flagship, the *Andrea Doria,* in 1952. The most luxurious passenger ship ever to sail on the southern route, she was thought to be the safest, incorporating all the latest safety devices including radar, a double hull, and eleven watertight compartments designed to localize the damage in case of an accident. But when she collided with the Swedish motorship *Stockholm* off Nantucket on June 25, 1956, her modern equipment could not save her—or forty-four of her passengers.

As the events of that night were reconstructed from conflicting testimony, the *Andrea Doria* was apparently proceeding westward through fog when she picked up the outward-bound *Stockholm* on her radar. Nautical rules of the road required that the ships pass port-to-port unless contrary signals indicated some other course. For reasons never fully explained, the *Andrea Doria* veered from her expected course into the path of the *Stockholm,* and the Swedish ship sliced into her starboard side, opening a gash seven decks high. She began to list immediately, making it impossible to lower most of the lifeboats. To the anguish of the ship's captain, many of his crew were the first to abandon ship.

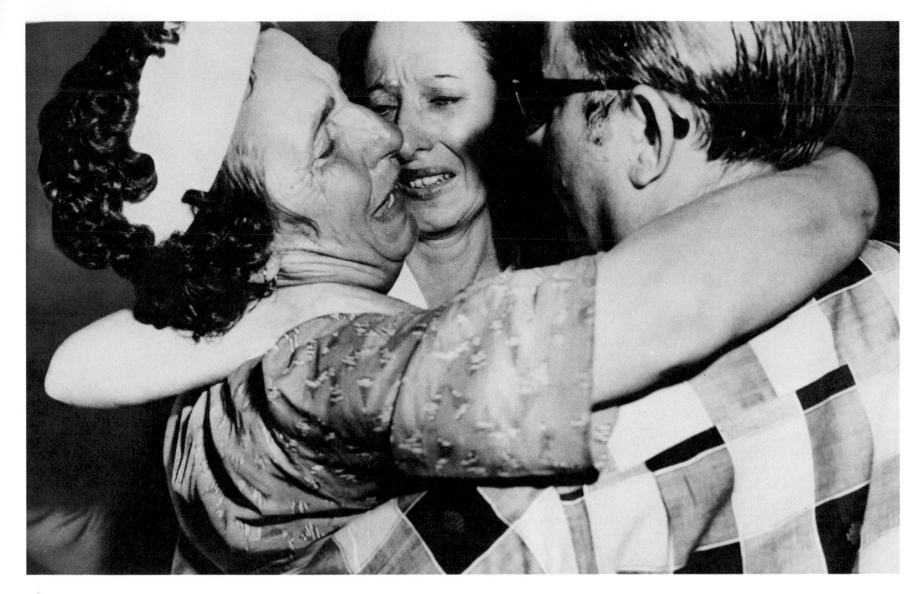

During her short career, the *Andrea Doria,* seen on the cover of the brochure (opposite, top) provided passengers with just what her brochures promised: "an experience that they will enjoy while they have it . . . one that they will never forget as long as they live." The words were all too ironic for the passengers and crew that survived the *Andrea Doria*'s collision with the *Stockholm.* As the photograph opposite (left) shows, the ship's vaunted stability failed in the crisis—perhaps due to improper distribution of ballast. By dawn she was listing at a forty degree angle. Fortunately, the seas were calm and most passengers were picked up by nearby ships. In the photo opposite (center), a lifeboat reaches the *Ile de France,* which had sped to the scene to offer assistance. Opposite below, the *Andrea Doria* heads for the deep, leaving a melancholy trail of deck chairs in her wake. Above, a distraught survivor is greeted on the dock after the ordeal. Meanwhile, the *Stockholm,* her icebreaker bow shredded by the impact, had limped toward New York carrying an additional 533 survivors. She is shown at right as she lay in dry dock for repairs.

The Italian Line launched a trio of spanking new ships in the 1960s—the *Leonardo da Vinci*, the *Michelangelo,* and the *Raffaello,* all of which proved well-suited to Caribbean service when Atlantic trade began to falter. The *Leonardo,* shown at anchor (left) in one of her tropical ports of call, and under way (opposite, right), boasted three swimming pools and decks tiered to give everyone space in the sun. Holland–America's *Rotterdam* (below) which entered service in 1959, offered such enticements as a week-long "Jazz and Jam" cruise to Nassau and the Bahamas, with "world famous jazz artists and historians." The *Caronia,* shown (opposite, left) in San Juan Harbor, was one of Cunard's most successful ships in her day.

A Splendid Fleet for the Trip to Nowhere

To "dance, and promenade, and smoke, and sing, and make love, and search the skies for constellations"— that's what people expect of a cruise, according to Mark Twain, who recorded his own experiences on an 1860s Middle East cruise in *The Innocents Abroad.* But if the reality didn't always live up to expectations (Twain's own trip became "a funeral excursion without a corpse"), the popularity of cruising has not been affected.

Beginning in the mid-nineteenth century as an occupation for the idle rich, the luxury cruise became, a century later, a favorite pastime for a multitude of vacationers. Although the transatlantic express liners were losing most of their business to the airlines, by the late 1950s whole new fleets of ships were starting to appear: ships designed to spend as much time cruising as crossing. Outdoor swimming pools and stem-to-stern air conditioning, largely useless on the North Atlantic, were standard features on the cruise liners.

This new approach was spectacularly successful. Mediterranean, Caribbean, and round-the-world cruises were filled to capacity; the more popular cruises were booked solid for months in advance. Meanwhile the number of ships making the transatlantic crossing continued to diminish every year.

The *Michelangelo* and the *Raffaello,* shown at their home berths in Genoa (below) and in an aerial view of the *Raffaello* (left), were launched in 1965. Each offered such amenities as nine swimming pools, a forty-bed hospital complete with psychiatrist and padded cell, and thirty bars and lounges. Not surprisingly, all this proved costly and, despite a loyal following, the Italian government phased the ships out in 1975. Swedish–American's *Gripsholm* (right) spent spring and summer on the Mediterranean and North Atlantic runs; from her winter home in Port Everglades, Florida, she made trips around South America. The *Alexander Pushkin* (opposite) is one of three Soviet cruise liners, all bearing proud Russian literary names.

In an effort to attract younger passengers, the *Independence* (above) was chartered for cruise service, with pay-as-you-eat meals and a redecorated "image" described as "psychedelic go-go" outside and "gay twenties" inside. The experiment failed and the once beautiful ship was shuttled off to retirement. Swedish–American's running mates, the motorships *Gripsholm* (left) and *Kungsholm,* shown in the three photos opposite, were designed from the start for cruising. Both sailed throughout the year, with cruises that lasted up to three months and sometimes girdled the globe. They provided live music, smorgasbords, and even the appropriate King Neptune investiture ceremonies for those crossing the Equator for the first time.

Requiem for the Giants

Sentenced to death, the *Ile de France* attained a certain dubious immortality when a film company leased her from Japanese salvagers for the purpose of sinking her on film. Honored with a Shinto requiem (opposite, top), she was rechristened the *Claridon* and was made the star performer in a 1960 movie called *The Last Voyage,* from which is taken the scene, at right, of passengers abandoning the burning ship. The *Claridon* was subsequently refloated and towed to the breakers in Osaka.

The *Queen Elizabeth* (opposite, right) went out in flames—whether by accident or arson is not known—as she lay in Hong Kong Harbor having been converted into a floating university.

The *Queen Mary* (above) changed her classification from ship to building in 1967, when she was permanently installed on a concrete foundation by her new owners, the City of Long Beach, California. Her final voyage, which carried her 14,500 miles from Southampton around Cape Horn to California, was run with more than one thousand American passengers aboard. She was then decommissioned and converted to a shore-front amusement center. Holland–America's *Nieuw Amsterdam* (opposite, left), the last of the pre–World War II liners in service, left New York on her final run in December, 1973, and was scrapped in Taiwan.

High hopes for the future of the transatlantic liner rode with the *France* and
the *QE2* on their maiden voyages (in
1962 and 1969 respectively). The festivi-
ties accorded the *Queen* on her first trip
out (below) were as tumultuous as they
could have been. For its part, the French
Line continued to offer "the longest
gangplank in the world" (opposite, right),
suggesting that to step aboard a French
liner was to be transported instantaneously
to France. But similarities with the heyday
of transatlantic travel ended there. In an
effort to reduce overhead, the rivals—
shown side by side in New York (opposite,
left)—shared terminals in New York and
Southampton and even worked in tandem,
running on alternating schedules.

Elegant Offspring of a Vanishing Breed

Entering a giant liner into service in the sixties, when
passenger revenues were declining, was a calculated
risk. But during that decade, two new liners
appeared: the *France* and the *Queen Elizabeth 2*. In
all likelihood, they would be the last ever built.

Ghosts haunted the yards where the *France* and
the *QE2* were launched. At St. Nazaire, people still
remembered when the *Ile de France* was built and
when the *Normandie* sailed forth to bring France its
only Blue Ribbon. At the John Brown Shipyards on
the Clyde lingered the legends of the *Lusitania,
Aquitania, Queen Mary,* and first *Queen Elizabeth.*

To many travelers it seemed inevitable that
the new ships could not compare in warmth and
character with their famous predecessors. But in size,
power, and popularity, the *France* and the *QE2*
were worthy descendants of their breed. The *France,*
1,035 feet overall, was the longest passenger ship
ever built, and could carry more people in a year
than the *Ile de France* and the *Normandie* combined.
The *QE2,* with her single stack and twin screws, was
designed to be the ultimate in computerized
efficiency. She developed more power on less fuel
than any other passenger ship; and although she
was only two-thirds their tonnage, she carried nearly
as many passengers as either of the old *Queen*s.

"To uphold and maintain the prestige of France on the Atlantic," was the charge given the French Line by Napoleon III in 1861. The *France,* entering service 101 years later, more than fulfilled that charge and was easily the most successful carrier of the decade. As suggested by the photos opposite, champagne was a must at every bon voyage party; and, in true French tradition, mealtimes were highpoints of every crossing. The *France*'s thirty-one-knot cruising speed, meanwhile, made for bracing strolls on the open decks.

The *France* ended service in 1974—due to the sudden quadrupling of oil prices and the French government's refusal to continue the ship's $20 million annual subsidy. A gay September departure (pictured at left and below) turned out to be the *France*'s last from the United States. In protest, the ship was seized by the crew outside Le Havre—as *The New York Times* reported (opposite, left)—and the passengers had to be taken off by car ferry. There were lengthy negotiations and brave words from the maritime union ("*The France* is France. And France is not for sale!"). But the government stuck by its decision. Three remaining crossings were canceled. The 6,100 people who held bookings had, it turned out, missed the boat; and, as the clipping at right also shows, they had very little else in the way of sea transport to choose from—nothing certainly, that came near to being a substitute for the regal *France.*

By NAN ROBERTSON
Special to The New York Times

Immediate End of Service By the France Is Ordered

PARIS, Sept. 18—The great luxury ship France is being pulled out of service immediately, the French Line announced here tonight.

A final trans-Atlantic round trip and two gala cruises that were to have taken place before the planned retirement date of Oct. 25 have been canceled.

The doomed and deficit-ridden liner was occupied by her crew last Wednesday night in an attempt to save their jobs and keep the France going.

About 1,300 passengers were evacuated to shore Thursday by a cross-channel car ferry after the crew took over the 66,000-ton liner and dropped anchor about three miles off

... ight and a supply of fresh water for the crew of 964.

Since the take-over last week, the company said, some bookings had been canceled because of the liner's uncertain future. Still other potential passengers had expressed fears of being stranded if they did not make alternative travel arrangements.

Augustin Gruennais, secretary general of the biggest French maritime union, retorted today that the French Line's decision to retire the ship at once "has changed nothing as far as our continuing struggle is concerned."

The line decided in July to decommission the 1,035-foot liner, the world's longest pas-...

Shipping/Mails

All Hours Given in Eastern Daylight Time

Incoming Passenger and Mail Ships

Tomorrow, Sept. 20

Ship	Passengers	From	Due	Will Dock
MAXIM GORKI, Wall St. Cruises		Bermuda	8 A.M.	W. 44th St.

Outgoing Passenger and Mail Ships

SAILING TODAY
Trans-Atlantic

FINN-AMER (Finn), Helsinki Oct. 5; sails from Port Newark, N.J.
MORMACBAY (Moore-McCormack), Durman Oct. 9, Mombassa 14 and Dar-Es-Salaam 24; sails from 23rd St., Brooklyn.
SL-McLEAN (Sea-Land), Rotterdam Sept. 24, Bremerhaven 26, Felixstowe 28 and Havre 29; sails from Elizabeth, N.J.
South America, West Indies, Etc.
GRIPSHOLM (Swed. Amer.), 13-day Colonial West Indies Cruise; sails 4:30 P.M. from W. 57th St.

SAILING TOMORROW
Trans-Atlantic
AMERICAN ACCORD (U.S. Lines), Havre

Oct. 2, Hamburg 7; sails from Elizabeth, N.J.
DART AMERICAN (Dart), Antwerp Sept. 30; sails from Global Marine Terminal, N.J.
ARYA SHAD (Arya), Khorramshahr Oct. 22 and Kuwait 24; sails from Joralemon St., Brooklyn.
South America, West Indies, Etc.
ATLANTIC SUN (Atlantic), Barbados Oct. 4, Georgetown 5; sails from 23rd St., Brooklyn.
CIUDAD DE ARMENIA (Grancolombiana), Buenaventura Sept. 30; sails from Furman St., Brooklyn.
PALAMEDES (Royal Netherlands), Puerto Limon Oct. 4; sails from 39th St., Brooklyn.

... there were only 8 to 10 per who defected."

The France is being run by ...

... is strewn with World War II wreckage, found an old mine near the France. It was re-...

"A great ship like the *Queen Elizabeth 2* must inevitably be looked upon as a sort of flagship for the nation," proclaimed Princess Margaret at the ship's launching. Sleekly modern in design, the *QE2* was built for cruising as well as for transatlantic liner service. She is seen at left in the waters off Barbados.

Unfortunately, she was plagued from the start by labor troubles, declining revenues, bomb threats, and mechanical failures. In the spring of 1974, she delivered a severe setback to her owners (no longer Cunard but a consortium known as Trafalgar Investments, Ltd.) when her boilers broke down during a "Sun and Fun Pigskin Cruise." All shipboard systems coasted to a halt, and her 1,630 passengers—hot under collars from lack of air conditioning and ice cubes—had to be transferred to another ship, carried to Bermuda, and flown home, with the entire cost of their fares returned.

Yet, for all her difficulties, the *QE2* has been successful both as a cruiser and as a liner. After the withdrawal of the *France* from service, the transatlantic crossing schedule of the *QE2* was expanded; and her future as a cruise ship remained bright. For a time, at least, elegant evenings in the main saloon (opposite, left) and quiet, contemplative days watching the sea (opposite, right) continued to be among the pleasures of shipboard life.

The view from the taffrail spans a world of ocean and one-hundred-fifty years of history—years when the broad Atlantic was bridged by a fleet of floating cities, mirrors of their age. Were they all resurrected and laid end to end, you might almost walk from Europe to America along their decks, passing through every period of design and meeting people from every level of society. For most liners, "finished with engines" has long since been rung down to the engine room. But aboard those few that remain on the North Atlantic, and aboard those others that spend their days cruising to exotic ports, something yet remains of the power, the elegance, and the sweet, unhurried pace of life aboard the great liners.

FINISHED WITH ENGINE
STOP
STAND BY
DEAD SLOW
SLOW
HALF
FULL
AHEAD
ASTERN
SLOW
HALF
FULL

Addenda

The chart below gives specifications for a few of the most famous North Atlantic passenger liners of the past one-hundred-fifty years. Ships that took the Blue Ribbon honors for the fastest crossing times are indicated with an asterisk (*). The number of engines in each ship is shown in parentheses after the type of engine.

Gross tonnage is based on the British measure, whereby a gross ton consists of 100 cubic feet of permanently enclosed passenger or cargo space. (Under the outmoded American system of 1865, gross tonnage included only those areas encompassed by the hull and the first deck attached to the hull.)

Twenty Great Liners and Their Specifications

Ship	Line	Maiden Voyage	Length (between perpendiculars)	Beam	Gross Tonnage	Funnels	Hull	Propulsion and Engine	Normal Speed
Savannah	Savannah Ship Co.	1819	98 feet	26 feet	320	1	wood	paddles; 1 cylinder	4 knots
*Great Western	Great Western	1838	212	35	1,340	1	wood	paddles; side lever (2)	9
Britannia	Cunard	1840	207	34	1,135	1	wood	paddles; side lever (2)	9
Great Britain	Great Western	1845	289	50	3,270	1	iron	screw; geared diagonal (4)	9
*Atlantic/Pacific/ Arctic/Baltic	Collins	1850	282	45	2,860	1	wood	paddles; side lever (2)	12
Great Eastern	Great Ship Co.	1860	680	83	18,915	5	iron	paddles & screw; oscillating (4) & horizontal (4)	12
*Kaiser Wilhelm der Grosse	North German Lloyd	1897	627	66	14,349	4	steel	2 screw; triple expansion (8)	22
*Mauretania/ Lusitania	Cunard	1907	762	88	31,938/ 31,550	4	steel	4 screw; turbine	25
Olympic/ Titanic	White Star	1911/1912	852	92	45,324/ 46,329	4	steel	3 screw; triple expansion (8), turbine	21
Leviathan (Vaterland)	United States (Hamburg–America)	1914	907	100	59,956	3	steel	4 screw; turbine	23
Ile de France	C.G.T.	1927	764	92	43,153	3	steel	4 screw; turbine	23
*Bremen	North German Lloyd	1929	899	102	51,656	2	steel	4 screw; geared turbine	27
Empress of Britain	Canadian Pacific	1931	733	98	42,348	3	steel	4 screw; geared turbine	24
*Rex	Italia	1932	833	97	51,062	2	steel	4 screw; geared turbine	28
*Normandie	C.G.T.	1935	981	118	82,799	3	steel	4 screw; turbo-electric	29
*Queen Mary	Cunard White Star	1936	975	119	80,774	3	steel	4 screw; geared turbine	29
Queen Elizabeth	Cunard White Star	1940 (1946)	987	118	83,673	2	steel	4 screw; geared turbine	29
*United States	United States	1952	917	102	53,329	2	steel	4 screw; geared turbine	33
France	C.G.T.	1962	1035 (over all)	110	66,348	2	steel	4 screw; geared turbine	31
Queen Elizabeth 2	Cunard	1968	963	105	65,863	1	steel	2 screw; geared turbine	28

The sea-lanes traveled by the great liners of the North Atlantic are indicated on the map below. Also shown are the primary American and European ports and the approximate southerly limit of the icebergs. It is due to the danger of icebergs that the sea-lanes to and from United States ports are located further south during the summer months than they are during the winter. In summer, icebergs appear on the North Atlantic in great profusion and travel far down the Canadian coast. The present summer tracks were fixed after the sinking of the *Titanic* in 1912, when they were shifted sixty miles south of their previous location.

The North Atlantic Seaway

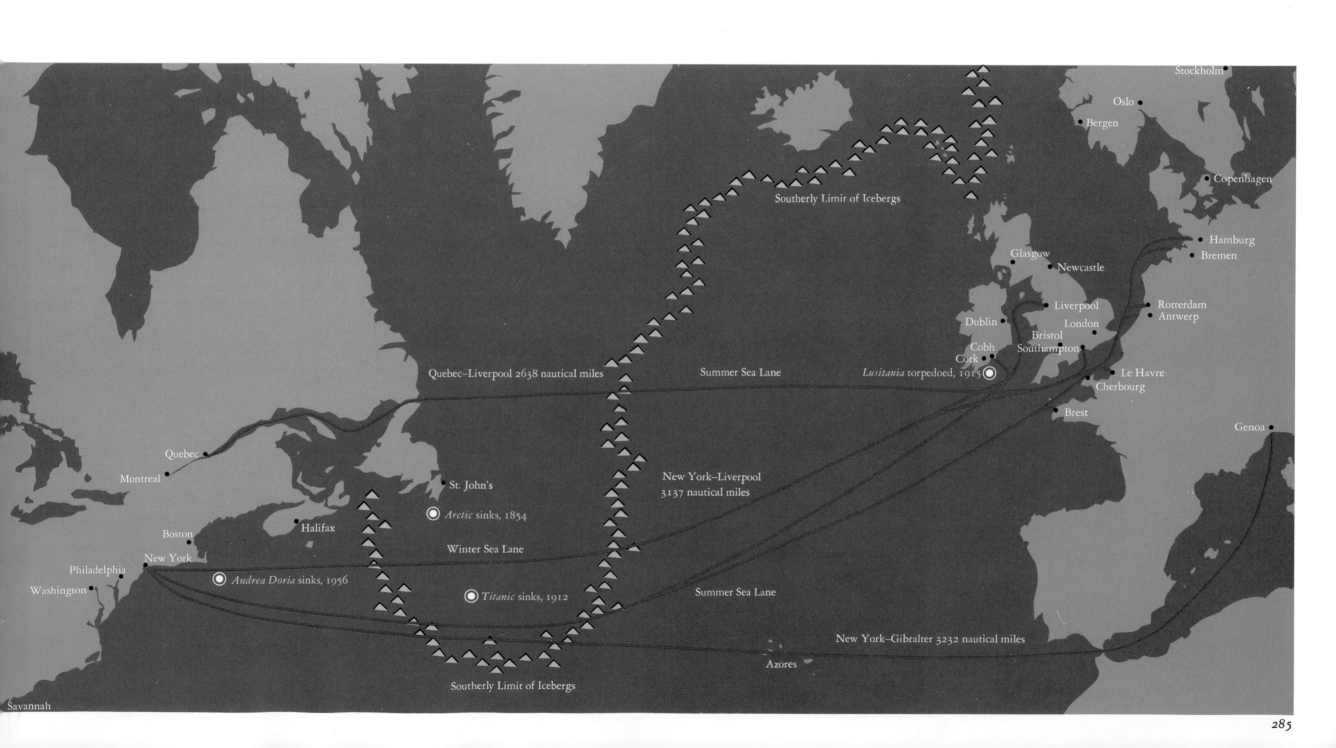

Stockholm

Oslo

Bergen

Copenhagen

Southerly Limit of Icebergs

Hamburg
Bremen

Glasgow
Newcastle

Rotterdam
Antwerp

Liverpool
London

Dublin
Bristol
Cobh   Southampton
Cork

Quebec–Liverpool 2638 nautical miles   Summer Sea Lane   *Lusitania* torpedoed, 1915 ⊙

Le Havre
Cherbourg

Brest

Genoa

Quebec

Montreal

St. John's

New York–Liverpool
3137 nautical miles

⊙ *Arctic* sinks, 1854

Boston

Halifax   Winter Sea Lane

New York

Philadelphia   ⊙ *Andrea Doria* sinks, 1956

Washington   ⊙ *Titanic* sinks, 1912   Summer Sea Lane

New York–Gibralter 3232 nautical miles

Azores

Southerly Limit of Icebergs

Savannah

Acknowledgments

The editors particularly wish to thank the following individuals and institutions for their assistance:

Peabody Museum of Salem, Massachusetts
   Markham W. Sexton, Staff Photographer
   Kathy M. Flynn, Photographic Assistant

The Mariners Museum, Newport News, Virginia
   John L. Lochhead, Librarian
   John O. Sands, Curator of Prints and Paintings
   William T. Radcliffe, Photographer

U.S. National Museum of History and Technology, Smithsonian Institution, Washington, D.C.
   Dr. John Hoffmann, Associate Curator of Mining and Curator of the Warshaw Collection of Business Americana
   Dr. Melvin R. Jackson, Curator of Marine Transportation
   Mary Ellen McCaffrey, Photographic Services

Compagnie Générale Transatlantique
   René Bouvard

Culver Pictures
   Robin Raffer

The New York Times
   John Morris
   Arthur Arons

Steamship Historical Society of America, Baltimore, Maryland
   James and Alice Wilson

New York Yacht Club
   Sohri Hohri, Librarian

Archives, Liverpool University; Cunard Line Ltd. Collection

Frank O. Braynard

John Malcolm Brinnin

Walter Lord

John K. Maxtone-Graham

Georgette Mewès

Daniel B. Morgan

Norman H. Morse

Ida J. Moss

David Rockefeller

Picture Credits

2 The Mariners Museum, Edwin Levick Collection. 8 Fritz Henle–Photo Researchers. 10 John Dominis–Life, 1974.

Chapter 1. 13 J.-B. Marestier, Memoires sur les bateaux des Etats-Unis d'Amérique, Paris, 1824; inset/Mary Seely Collection. 14 The Science Museum, London. 15 BL/Watercraft Collection, Smithsonian Institution; TM/The Franklin Institute, Philadelphia; TR/The Mariners Museum. 16 L/I. N. Phelps Stokes Collection, New York Public Library; R/Picture Collection, New York Public Library. 17 both L/The Mariners Museum; M/Watercraft Collection, Smithsonian Institution; R/Radio Times Hulton Picture Library. 18 both/Watercraft Collection, Smithsonian Institution. 19 T/The Mariners Museum; B/Georgia Historical Society. 20 Watercraft Collection, Smithsonian Institution. 21 both T/Georgia Historical Society; BL/The Times, London, June 30, 1819; BM/Mary Seely Collection. 22 L/Musée du Québec; TR/Peabody Museum of Salem; BM/National Maritime Museum, London. 23 T/National Portrait Gallery, London; B/Sterling Memorial Library, Yale University. 24 L/The Mariners Museum; R/Culver Pictures. 25 L/Hull Maritime Museum; TM/The Science Museum, London. 26 L/The Science Museum, London; M/Peabody Museum of Salem; R/The Granger Collection. 27 L/New-York Historical Society; TR/I. N. Phelps Stokes Collection, New York Public Library; BR/The Mariners Museum. 28 L/The Science Museum, London; 28–29 The Mariners Museum.

Chapter 2. 31 The Mariners Museum, Eldredge Collection. 32–33 all/G.P.O. Records Room, London. 34 L/The Mariners Museum; R/The Science Museum, London. 35 I.N. Phelps Stokes Collection, New York Public Library. 36 L/The Mariners Museum, Eldredge Collection; R/Warshaw Collection, Smithsonian Institution. 37 T/Public Archives of Nova Scotia–Stewart Bale, Ltd.; BL/Peabody Museum of Salem; BR/G.P.O. Records Room, London. 38 The Mariners Museum. 39 L/The Bostonian Society; all M/Archives, Liverpool University; R/The Mariners Museum. 40–41 National Maritime Museum, London. 41 T/The Mariners Museum; B/Warshaw Collection, Smithsonian Institution. 42 Peabody Museum of Salem. 43 all/The Mariners Museum. 44 Compagnie Générale Transatlantique. 45 L/Harper's Monthly, July, 1870; R/Compagnie Générale Transatlantique. 46 both/Culver Pictures. 47 The Mariners Museum. 48 Museum of the City of New York. 49 BL and T/Culver Pictures; BR/Peabody Museum of Salem. 50 L/Harper's Monthly, February, 1892; TM/The Mariners Museum, Eldredge Collection; BM/The Lantern, March 13, 1852; R/Warshaw Collection, Smithsonian Institution. 51 both/Watercraft Collection, Smithsonian Institution. 52 L/The Mariners Museum. 52–53 Walter Lord Collection. 54 all/The Science Museum, London. 55 Illustrated London News, Sept. 24, 1859. 56 The Mariners Museum. 57 T/The Science Museum, London; M and B/Radio Times Hulton Picture Library. 58 L/The Science Museum, London; R/Keystone Press. 59 L/Brunel University Library; R/Watercraft Collection, Smithsonian Institution; 60–61 all/Watercraft Collection, Smithsonian Institution. 62 The Mariners Museum. 63 L/Radio Times Hulton Picture Library; R/Brunel University Library. 64 TL/Pea-

body Museum of Salem; BL/Mary Evans Picture Library; R/Warshaw Collection, Smithsonian Institution. 65 Peabody Museum of Salem.

Chapter 3. 67 L/Birmingham Museum and Art Gallery; TR/Museum of the City of New York, Byron Collection; BR/New York Public Library. 68 Museum of the City of New York. 69 TL/Staatsbibliothek, Berlin; TM/Minnesota Historical Society; R/New-York Historical Society. 70 Staatsbibliothek, Berlin. 71 L/Staatsbibliothek, Berlin; both R/Mary Evans Picture Library. 72 L/Peabody Museum of Salem; R/Merseyside County Museums, Liverpool. 73 L/Merseyside County Museums, Liverpool; both R/The Mariners Museum. 74 both/The Mariners Museum. 75 L/Musée de la Marine, Paris; TR/The Mariners Museum; BR/Compagnie Générale Transatlantique. 76 L/The Mansell Collection; TR/Staatsbibliothek, Berlin; BR/National Maritime Museum, London. 77 Culver Pictures. 78 Culver Pictures. 79 L/Mary Evans Picture Library; R/Staatsbibliothek, Berlin. 80 L/Staatsbibliothek, Berlin; R/The Graphic, March 12, 1870. 81 TL/Courtesy Roy Anderson; BL/Peabody Museum of Salem; R/Warshaw Collection, Smithsonian Institution. 82 L/Mary Evans Picture Library; R/Harper's Monthly, March, 1871. 83 L/Warshaw Collection, Smithsonian Institution; R/Library of Congress. 84–85 Library of Congress, Edwin Levick photograph. 86 Compagnie Générale Transatlantique. 87 L/Riksutställningar–Swedish Traveling Exhibitions; R/Ullstein. 88 L/The Mariners Museum; R/Culver Pictures. 89 Museum of the City of New York. 90 both/Compagnie Générale Transatlantique. 91 all/Frank O. Braynard Collection. 92 L/The

Mariners Museum, Edwin Levick Collection. 92–93 Library of Congress. 93 R/The Mariners Museum, Edwin Levick Collection. 94 L/U.S. Immigration & Naturalization Service; both R/Culver Pictures. 95 TL/The Granger Collection; BL/UPI; BM/George Eastman House, Lewis Hine photograph; all others/Culver Pictures. 96 L/Culver Pictures. 96–97 Library of Congress.

Chapter 4. 99 The Granger Collection. 100 Courtesy John Kemble. 101 L/The Mansell Collection; M/Peabody Museum of Salem; R/The Mariners Museum. 102 T/Peabody Museum of Salem; all B/*Harper's Monthly,* August, 1886. 103 both L/The Mariners Museum, Eldredge Collection; R/Museum of the City of New York. 104 L/Peabody Museum of Salem; TR/Merseyside County Museums, Liverpool; MR and BR/ National Maritime Museum, London. 105 National Maritime Museum, London. 106 The Bettmann Archive. 107 L/The Mansell Collection; R/The Mariners Museum. 108 L/The Mariners Museum, Eldredge Collection. 108–109 Peabody Museum of Salem. 109 T/Watercraft Collection, Smithsonian Institution (Cropley Collection). 110 Tre Tryckare, *The Lore of Ships,* 1963. 111 Peabody Museum of Salem. 112 TL/Peabody Museum of Salem; BL/The Mariners Museum, Eldredge Collection; TR/The Mariners Museum; R/both/Peabody Museum of Salem. 114 L and M/ Staatsbibliothek, Berlin; R/The Mariners Museum, Eldredge Collection. 115 L/ Georgette Mewès Collection; R/Museum of the City of New York, Byron Collection. 116 both T/Georgette Mewès Collection; B/Staatsbibliothek, Berlin. 117 L/ Courtesy John Malcolm Brinnin; R/Frank O. Braynard Collection.

Chapter 5. 119 T/British Crown Copyright. The Science Museum, London; B/ The Mariners Museum. 120 both/Culver Pictures. 121 both/The Science Museum, London. 122 T/Tre Tryckare, *The Lore of Ships,* 1963; BL/The Science Museum, London; BR/Swan Hunter Group, Ltd. 123 T and BM/Norman H. Morse Collection; BL/*The Shipbuilder;* BR/Swan Hunter Group, Ltd. 124 TL/*The Shipbuilder;* TM/Norman H. Morse Collection. 124–125 *The Shipbuilder.* 126–127 all/Peabody Museum of Salem. 128 TL/Brown Brothers; BL/Peabody Museum of Salem; R/Watercraft Collection, Smithsonian Institution. 129 T/Radio Times Hulton Picture Library; B/Peabody Museum of Salem. 130 T/Peabody Museum of Salem; B/Brown Brothers. 131 L/The Mariners Museum; both R/The Mariners Museum, Edwin Levick Collection. 132–133 John D. Rockefeller photograph from Rockefeller Family Archives; all others/ Culver Pictures. 134 TL/Brown Brothers; BL/Radio Times Hulton Picture Library; TR/Steamship Historical Society of America; BR/Peabody Museum of Salem. 135 Peabody Museum of Salem. 136–137 both/Walter Lord Collection. 138 TL/ Merseyside County Museums, Liverpool; ML/Peabody Museum of Salem; BL and TM/Popperfoto; BR/*Illustrated London News,* 1912. 139 both/ Brown Brothers. 140 L/*Illustrated London News,* May 4, 1912; TR/Peabody Museum of Salem; MR/Culver Pictures; BR/Underwood & Underwood. 141 L/*Overture* Magazine, 1912; M/Underwood & Underwood; R/ Walter Lord Collection. 142 Morris Rosenfeld. 143 L/Compagnie Générale Transatlantique; TR/Peabody Museum of Salem; BR/Staatsbibliothek, Berlin. 144 L/Museum of the City of New York,

Byron Collection; both R/Brown Brothers. 145 L and TR/Compagnie Générale Transatlantique; BR/Cunard, Ltd. 146 L/National Archives; R/Frank O. Braynard Collection. 147 L/Peabody Museum of Salem; R/Frank O. Braynard Collection.

Chapter 6. 149 Merseyside County Museums, Liverpool–Stewart Balc, Ltd. photograph. 150–151 National Archives. 151 B and R/Peabody Museum of Salem. 152 L/Steamship Historical Society of America; R/The Mariners Museum. 153 National Archives. 154–155 all/The Mariners Museum. 156 L/Culver Pictures. 156–157 Peabody Museum of Salem. 157 T and R/Brown Brothers. 158–159 all/ Peabody Museum of Salem. 160 T/Radio Times Hulton Picture Library; B/The Mansell Collection. 160–161 Culver Pictures. 161 TL/Brown Brothers; R/ *Literary Digest,* May 22, 1915. 162 L/National Archives; R/Paul Thompson. 163 Print Room, Victoria and Albert Museum. 164 L/National Archives; R/ The Mariners Museum. 165 T/Imperial War Museum; B/Peabody Museum of Salem. 166 all/Frank O. Braynard Collection. 167 TL/National Archives; BL/*The New York Times;* R/Cunard, Ltd. 168 L/National Archives; TR/Peabody Museum of Salem; BR/Compagnie Générale Transatlantique. 169 both/Peabody Museum of Salem.

Chapter 7. 171 Compagnie Générale Transatlantique. 172 Warshaw Collection, Smithsonian Institution. 173 BL/The Mariners Museum, Edwin Levick Collection; TL and TM/Warshaw Collection, Smithsonian Institution; TR/Frank O. Braynard Collection. 174 TR/The Mariners Museum; all others/Peabody Museum of Salem. 175 L/Peabody Museum

of Salem; M/The Mariners Museum; R/ Norman H. Morse Collection. 176 TL and B/The Mariners Museum; TR/Brown Brothers. 177 L/The Mariners Museum, Edwin Levick Collection; R/Norman H. Morse Collection. 178 L/Collection Viollet; TR/Compagnie Générale Transatlantique; BR/Paul Thompson. 179 L/Peabody Museum of Salem; R/ Cunard, Ltd. 180 *The New York Times.* 181 L/Holland–America Line; M/Norman H. Morse Collection; R/National Archives. 182 L/Compagnie Générale Transatlantique. 182–183 both/Norman H. Morse Collection. 184 L/Holland– America Line; R/UPI. 185 L/Norman H. Morse Collection; TM/Archives, Liverpool University; M/Keystone Press; BM/Peabody Museum of Salem; R/The Mariners Museum. 186–187 Mme Curie photograph from The Mariners Museum, Edwin Levick Collection; Tom Mix photograph from Charles T. Spedding, *Reminiscence of Transatlantic Travellers,* 1926; all others/Culver Pictures. 188 Holland–America Line. 189 L/The Mansell Collection; TM/Radio Times Hulton Picture Library; BM/Peabody Museum of Salem; R/National Archives. 190 TL and BR/Radio Times Hulton Picture Library; BL/Peabody Museum of Salem; TR/Archives, Liverpool University. 191 *The New York Times.* 192 TL/The Mansell Collection; BL/The Mariners Museum; M/Herbert Photos, Inc.; BR/The Mariners Museum, Edwin Levick Collection. 193 M/Radio Times Hulton Picture Library; BL/Museum of the City of New York, Byron Collection; R/Frank O. Braynard Collection. 194 L/ Culver Pictures. 194–195 Holland–America Line. 195 TL/Compagnie Générale Transatlantique; TR/Museum of the City

of New York, Byron Collection; BR/ Peabody Museum of Salem. 196–197 and 197 M/The Mariners Museum; R/Compagnie Générale Transatlantique.

Chapter 8. 199 L/Radio Times Hulton Picture Library; R/Lords Gallery, London–BPC Picture Library. 200 New York *Herald Tribune,* July 10, 1938. 201 TL/ Compagnie Générale Transatlantique; BL/*The New York Times;* R/Norman H. Morse Collection. 202 L/Norman H. Morse Collection; R/Staatsbibliothek, Berlin. 203 TL/Norman H. Morse Collection; BL/The Mariners Museum; R/UPI. 204 both/Peabody Museum of Salem. 205 TL and R/Eric Solomon; BL/Warshaw Collection, Smithsonian Institution. 206 T/Wide World; B/The Mariners Museum. 207 L/The Italian Line; R/The Mariners Museum. 208–209 all/The Mariners Museum. 210–211 all/*The New York Times.* 212 all/The Mariners Museum. 213 The Mariners Museum. 214 TL/Museum of the City of New York, Byron Collection; BL/Compagnie Générale Transatlantique. 214–215 Keystone Press. 215 TR/Compagnie Générale Transatlantique; BR/Roger Schall. 216–217 King Saud photograph courtesy Daniel B. Morgan; Thomas Mann photograph courtesy Holland–America Line; all others/Culver Pictures. 218 Cunard, Ltd. 219 Aerial Exploration, Inc. 220 both L/Radio Times Hulton Picture Library; R/Archives, Liverpool University–Stewart Bale, Ltd. photograph. 221 L/Archives, Liverpool University; TR/Graphic Photos; BR/The Mariners Museum. 222–23 *Illustrated London News,* on permanent loan to the Science Museum, London. 224 L/Archives, Liverpool University, courtesy Southampton Museum; both R/Radio Times Hulton

Selected Bibliography

Picture Library. **225** L/Cunard, Ltd.– Stewart Bale, Ltd.; R/Radio Times Hulton Picture Library. **226** L/Cunard, Ltd.– W. A. Probst; R/Holland–America Line. **226–227** Canadian Pacific. **227** R/Frank O. Braynard Collection.

Chapter 9. 229 Holland–America Line. **230** *The New York Times.* **231** L/Frank O. Braynard Collection; R/Norman H. Morse Collection. **232** L/Lionel Green– Frederic Lewis, Inc. **232–233** Holland– America Line. **233** R/UPI. **234** all and **234– 235**/*The New York Times.* **235** TL/Water-craft Collection, Smithsonian Institution (Cropley Collection); R/National Archives. **236** T/Imperial War Museum; both B/*The New York Times.* **237** both/ Wide World. **238** T//National Archives; BL/Peabody Museum of Salem. **238–239** National Archives. **239** both R/The Mariners Museum, Robert J. Russell Collection. **240** both L/Imperial War Museum. **240–241** T/Peabody Museum of Salem; B/National Archives. **241** M/*The Shipbuilder;* R/Frank O. Bray-nard Collection. **242** all/Imperial War Museum. **243** L/National Archives; R/ Imperial War Museum. **244** L/Stewart Bale, Ltd.; R/Michael B. Wray Collection. **245** L/Imperial War Museum; R/National Archives. **246** both/*The New York Times.* **246–247** Archives, Liverpool University.

Chapter 10. 249 Farrell Grehan–Photo Researchers. **250** Randolph Barton Collection. **251** CGT ashtray from William Waters Collection; others from George H. Dare Collection; B/UPI. **252** L/Kevin Scott–FPG; R/Dick Davis–Photo Researchers. **253** T/Erich Hartmann– Magnum; B/Henri Dauman. **254** T/288

Randolph Barton; B/C. Spanton Ash-down. **255** L/Lee Lockwood–Black Star; R/Randolph Barton. **256** TL and MR/ Archives, Liverpool University; BL/Henri Dauman; TR and BR/Erich Hartmann– Magnum. **257** L/Erich Hartmann– Magnum; TR/Archives, Liverpool Uni-versity; BR/Radio Times Hulton Picture Library. **258** T/The Mariners Museum. **258–259** The Mariners Museum, William T. Radcliffe photograph. **259** R/Randolph Barton. **260** TM/*The New York Times;* others/The Mariners Museum. **260–261** The Mariners Museum. **261** R/*The New York Times.* **262** L/Newport News Shipbuilding & Drydock Co.; M/ The Mariners Museum; R/Patrick A. Burns. **263** Andreas Feininger. **264** L/ Brown Brothers; TM/*The New York Times;* BM/Peabody Museum of Salem, by permission of the Hearst Corp.; TR/ The Mariners Museum, Ellsworth Philip Collection. **265** both/*The New York Times.* **266** L/J. Alex Langley–DPI; R/ Eric Carle–Shostal. **267** L/Richard Davis– DPI; R/Flying Camera–DPI. **268** L/ Werner Wolff–Black Star; M/Publifoto– Black Star; R/Al Esmont–Photo Re-searchers. **269** Richard Divald–Photo Researchers. **270** T/Yale Joel–Time–Life; B/Dana Brown–Alpha. **271** both L/Erich Hartmann–Magnum; R/Dana Brown– FPG. **272** L/Holland–America Line; TR/ Compagnie Générale Transatlantique; BR/UPI. **273** T/Carlos Elmer–FPG; B/ Movie Star News. **274** Larry Mulvehill– Photo Researchers. **275** L/UPI; R/Mary M. Thacher–Photo Researchers. **276** both/ William Waters. **277** ML and TR/Elliott Erwitt–Magnum; BL/*The New York Times,* Sept. 19, 1974; BR/Allyn Baum– *The New York Times.* **278** R. V. Fuschetto–Photo Researchers. **279** L/

Larry Morris–*The New York Times;* R/Chris Clarke–Photo Researchers. **280** Henry Monroe–DPI. **281** Don Hogan Charles–*The New York Times.* **285** Map by Robert Ritter.

Albion, Robert G. *The Rise of New York Port, 1815–1860.* New York, 1939, 1970.
Anderson, Roy. *White Star.* Prescot, Lancashire, 1964.
Armstrong, Warren. *Atlantic Highway.* New York, 1961.
Baker, William A. *From Paddle Wheel to Nuclear Ship.* London, 1965.
Bemsted, C. R. *The Atlantic Ferry.* London, 1936.
Bonsor, N. R. P. *North Atlantic Seaway.* Prescot, Lancashire, 1955.
Bowen, Frank. *A Century of Atlantic Travel.* Boston, 1930.
Bowen, Frank, and H. Parker, *Mail and Passenger Steamships of the 19th Century.* London, 1928.
Braynard, Frank O. *Lives of the Liners.* New York, 1947.
——. *S. S. Savannah.* Athens, Georgia, 1963.
——. *The Leviathan.* New York, 1972.
Brinnin, John Malcolm. *The Sway of the Grand Saloon.* New York, 1971.
Bunting, W. H. *Portrait of a Port: Boston, 1852 to 1914.* Cambridge, Massachu-setts, 1970.
Chapelle, Howard I. "The Pioneer Steam-ship Savannah," *Contributions from the Museum of History and Technology, U.S. National Museum Collection 228, Part 3.* Washington, D.C., 1961.
Chatterton, E. Keble. *Steamships and Their Story.* London, 1910.
Dugan, James. *The Great Iron Ship.* New York, 1953.
Dunn, Laurence. *Famous Liners of the Past—Belfast Built.* London, 1964.
——. *Passenger Liners.* London, 1961.
——. *Ship Recognition.* London, 1954.
Durant, J., and A. Durant. *A Picture His-*

tory of American Ships. New York, 1953.
Fraser–Macdonald, A. *Our Ocean Rail-ways.* London, 1893.
Gibbs, C. R. Vernon. *Passenger Liners of the Western Ocean.* London, 1952.
Greenhill, Basil, and Giffard, Ann. *Travelling by Sea in the Nineteenth Century.* London, 1972.
Handlin, Oscar. *The Uprooted.* Boston, 1951, 1973.
Hoff, Rhoda. *America's Immigrants.* New York, 1967.
Lord, Walter. *A Night to Remember.* New York, 1955.
Maxtone-Graham, John. *The Only Way to Cross.* New York, 1972.
Morrison, John H. *History of American Steam Navigation.* New York, 1903, 1958.
Outwaite, Leonard. *The Atlantic.* New York, 1957.
Rowland, K. T. *Steam at Sea.* Newton Abbot, Devonshire, 1970.
Spratt, H. P. *Outline History of Trans-atlantic Paddle Steamers.* Glasgow, 1951.
——. *Outline History of Transatlantic Steam Navigation.* London, 1950.
Staff, Frank. *The Transatlantic Mail.* New York, 1956.
Talbot, Frederick A. *Steamship Conquest of the World.* London, 1912.
Tre Tryckare, Pub. *The Lore of Ships.* Göteborg, Sweden, 1963.
Tute, Warren. *Atlantic Conquest.* Toronto, 1962.
Tyler, David B. *Steam Conquers the Atlantic.* New York, 1939.
Weisberger, Bernard. *The American Heritage History of the American People.* New York, 1971.